GLITTERING MISERY

Family of Captain Charles Grierson, 10th Cavalry, taken at Fort Clark, Texas, late 1890's. From left to right, John Charles, Alice Kirk, Daisy and Sarah Joy Grierson. Misses Alice and Sarah reside in Los Angeles. Courtesy Fort Davis National Historic Site, Fort Davis, Texas.

GLITTERING MISERY

Dependents of the Indian Fighting Army

PATRICIA Y. STALLARD

Presidio Press · The Old Army Press

Library of Congress Catalog Card Number: 77-94525

ISBN: 0-88342-054-6 (hard cover)
ISBN: 0-88342-239-5 (soft cover)

Printed in The United States

Cover & Book Design by Leslie A. Johnston

A MICHAEL J. KOURY BOOK

Co-published by

PRESIDIO PRESS
SAN RAFAEL · CALIFORNIA

FORT COLLINS · COLORADO

CONTENTS

To Don Rickey, Jr., who set the guidons and blazed the trail, and to my son Will who, hopefully, will follow.

PREFACE

The contributions made by members of the Indian-Fighting Army have been recorded in countless historical and fictional accounts, but those of their dependents have hardly been mentioned, or only mentioned in passing. The women and children of the Western Army faced the same hardships, dared the same dangers, and experienced the same feelings of frustration and alienation as did the soldiers. They shared life on a hostile frontier, far removed from the comfort of friends and relatives left back East, and actively participated in the thankless chore of making the frontier safe for farmers and townsmen.

Although several wives such as Martha Summerhayes and Elizabeth Custer, and Captain Charles King wrote about the domestic life of army dependents, only recently has interest in the home life of the Frontier Army been evident. Perhaps this new interest is a product of the Women's Movement or the outcome of research into the history of the family. Whatever the cause, more sources are being discovered among state historical collections and especially at National Historic Sites where descendents of the Indian-Fighting Army have deposited family papers.

This work is, therefore, an attempt to relate the lives of army dependents during the period 1865-1898, when the American Army was primarily involved in internal pacification. The manuscript is not intended as a history of the Indian Wars — others have done that already and with far greater skill. And it is not intended to be the complete story of the dependents of the Western Army since such a task is impossible by any historian's standards and new sources are still being located. What the work does provide in addition to a glimpse of the lives of these "camp followers" is a starting point for future research.

Among those to whom a debt of gratitude is owed are the army women who kept diaries, wrote memoirs and instilled in their children a sense of history along with a sense of purpose. Among those descendents are Miss Dorothy Ronayne, Miss Mariana Lewis, Misses Alice Kirk and Sarah Joy Grierson, and Colonel Adna Chaffee Hamilton who have graciously shared their families' histories with me.

Three historians directed the original research and to them I am greatly indebted: Dr. Emmett M. Essin was the chairman of my thesis committee and provided the guidance necessary for completion of that undertaking; the late Dr. Robert G. Crawford lent moral support and epitomized the humane scholar; and Dr. Morton A. Brown served as arbiter of correct English usage and as the model of a judicious mind.

I am also grateful to Dr. Don Rickey, Jr., who had originally intended to include a chapter about army dependents in his *Forty Miles a Day on Beans and Hay*, but who made his notes and sources available to me. Colonel Herbert M. Hart, U.S. Marine Corps, loaned me several rare and valuable books which greatly expedited my research. Dr. B.F. Cooling, Mr. William Slonaker, and Dr. Richard Sommers aided my research at the U.S. Army Military History Institute and suggested other sources.

Mrs. Sara D. Jackson of the National Historical Publications Commission provided information about Lieutenant Henry O. Flipper and her characteristic kindness and enthusiasm. Dale Floyd and Dr. Elaine Everly, both of the National Archives' Navy and Old Army Branch have graciously continued to answer my requests for material. Ms. Wilma Short of Arlington, Virginia and Mrs. Dina Tabaz of Alexandria, Virginia furnished shelter, aid and comfort, and research assistance.

Among those who must be acknowledged for providing photographs of the dependents of the Indian-Fighting Army are: John Phillip Langellier of the Presidio of San Francisco, Douglas McChristian of Fort Laramie National Historic Site, Ms. Mary Williams of Fort Davis National Historic Site, Ms. Lynda S. Roper of the U.S. Army Field Artillery and Fort Sill Museum, and the staff of Fort Huachuca Museum.

The Inter-Library Loan Departments of both East Tennessee State University and the University of Tennessee-Knoxville cheerfully processed my numerous requests.

Finally, my husband and son ignored traditional sex roles and created the opportunity for me to undertake the project.

All these individuals and many others not named generously shared their time, expertise, and enthusiasm, but I alone am responsible for any errors which may occur within the text.

Patricia Yeary Stallard

Flatwoods, Virginia
June 1977

No. 1292. FORT MEADE.
. Fort Meade, Dak., Bear Butte, 6 mile
distant. Located in "Black Hills."
(Photo and copyright by Grabill, '88.)

View of Fort Meade, Dakota Territory in 1888, showing typical layout of the western frontier forts. Courtesy U.S. Army Military History Institute, Carlisle Barracks, Pennsylvania.

1

THE DISMAL YEARS
"The Western Army could represent nothing more than a thin blue line on a vast tract of land."

ust as their British predecessors followed the Light Brigade to Balaclava, American women returned to the frontier with the Indian-Fighting Army.[2] Of course, some army dependents had remained in the trans-Mississippi West throughout the period of the Civil War; but, with the closing of that conflict and the return of the Regular Army to the frontier, women and children moved westward in far greater numbers. General William T. Sherman encouraged army wives along that line when he met a group of them in St. Louis just prior to his third inspection of the West in 1866. General Sherman urged the ladies to accompany their husbands on their new western assignments. Speaking optimistically, the officer predicted that not only would garrison life on the frontier prove "healthful and pleasant" for all army dependents, but also they need have no fears about the hostile Indians. Sherman advised the women to "take with them all the needed comforts for a . . . life in the newly opened country. . . ."[3] Although a superior commanding officer, Sherman misinterpreted the immediate future. His over-optimistic predictions were not realized until the twentieth century. Throughout the period of the Indian Wars, life for army dependents in the trans-Mississippi West was not so healthful, pleasant, nor always peaceful. Those women and children who followed the western army experienced the physical hardships attendant with life upon an unsettled frontier. During the period 1865-1898, they ventured forth into a hostile environment; because within those years the Regulars engaged in "943 actions in twelve separate campaigns and numerous local incidents."[4]

11

Army wives accompanied their soldiers to the frontier for many reasons; but, primarily, they went out of love and a sense of duty. The women considered their role as that of a refuge where their husbands could find comfort and the reassurance that the task they had undertaken was justified. Often frustrated soldiers declared that the pacification of the frontier was a most difficult, thankless chore made even more troublesome by a Congress that kept cutting back the strength of the Regular Army. Because of the expanse of territory and the elusiveness of the foe, the military men realized that the "western army could represent nothing more than a thin blue line on a vast tract of land."[5] Army dependents traveled west determined to assist the army in this seemingly impossible endeavor.

The dependents who followed the army to the frontier did not always find pleasant and comfortable posts; however, forts located on the Pacific Coast and in the more settled regions of the western interior offered all the social amenities. For the most part, army dependents found mere sites for garrisons that had to be built by the soldiers themselves. Consequently, they lived in tents, adobe huts, and bug-infested log cabins. The women exerted every effort and taxed their creativity to provide pleasant home atmospheres. Those who could not endure the bleakness of the frontier and the stresses of life under uncertain conditions quickly became disillusioned with army life and returned East. The ones who remained made the meager supplies provided by the post quartermasters suffice and created a reasonable homelife. They could have languished on the posts so far removed from civilization, but they chose instead to face the situation and to seek fulfillment in being good army wives.

Generally, army children found frontier life exhilarating. Athough they were subject to the usual complement of childhood diseases, the fresh air and openness of the West seemed to have a salutary effect on their health. Young boys, especially, found a paradise on the frontier. Their playground stretched for miles, and they could do just about everything boys dream of doing.[6] They learned to ride and to shoot and enjoyed the companionship of the enlisted men and Agency Indians. The major drawback to growing up on the frontier was the lack of adequate educational facilities, and army parents often decided to send their children away to boarding schools.

The only women associated with the army who received official recognition were the company laundresses who had been

12

allowed to accompany the troops since 1802. The laundresses received housing, a daily ration, fuel, and the services of the post surgeon in addition to their pay for doing the company wash. In reality, they gave more than they received because they fulfilled many useful functions on post. They provided a homelife for their husbands who usually were the senior non-commissioned officers. The laundresses also nursed the sick and helped the officers' families in times of need. Their lives proved difficult, and sometimes their manners, coarse; but they deserve better treatment than they have received at the hands of popular historians.

The frontier army also attracted prostitutes who have always followed soldiers. These "camp followers" lived inside the garrisons, at the "hog ranches" just outside the military reservations, or in the wide-open towns that sprang up near the frontier posts. Because soldiers had little money to spend, they patronized some of the most decrepit and diseased prostitutes. Consequently, the army waged a constant battle against the spread of venereal diseases.

Many different types of women, from the socialite daughters of old established families to the humblest Irish immigrants who found employment as company laundresses, followed the Indian-Fighting Army west. They and their children participated in the last great task of continental expansion — the pacification of the Western Indian tribes. These dependents willingly accompanied the army beyond the bounds of civilization and endured a life best characterized by the phrase, "Glittering Misery."[7]

The author
Elizabeth J. Reynolds Burt
1862

Mrs. Elizabeth J. Reynolds Burt, wife of then Lieutenant A.S. Burt and mother of Reynolds Burt. Courtesy Fort Laramie National Historic Site, Wyoming.

2

THE OFFICERS' LADIES
"I had cast my lot with a soldier and where he was, was home to me."

soldier serving on the frontier offered the following words of warning to all young ladies who fell under the spell of brass buttons:

> Let all young ladies who are dazzled with the glare of
> gilt buttons at some of the fashionable parties on East,
> bear these and other deprivations in mind before saying
> "yes" to the fascinating Sons of Mars.[2]

Martha Dunham, welcomed home from Germany by family and friends early in 1874, received a most enthusiastic reception from Second Lieutenant Jack Summerhayes. So hearty was his greeting that she wrote: "I concluded the only thing to do was to join the Army myself."[3] Martha Summerhayes spoke for all the women who followed their men westward during the period of the Indian Wars: they had cast their lots with soldiers and wherever their men traveled they would follow. Elizabeth Burt who accompanied her husband throughout his military career spanning forty years explained her concept of duty: "He and I discussed the matter and agreed that wherever orders took him, baby and I would go too."[4]

Officers' wives accompanied their husbands for the same reasons women have ventured forth on any new frontier: love, a sense of duty, the need to provide comfort and cheerful surroundings, and the desire to be where they felt most needed. Since most officers' ladies came from upper middle-class eastern homes, they held, for the most part, romantic concepts of life on the frontier among Cooper's Noble Savages. For an officer's wife, service in the trans-Mississippi West during the period 1865-1898, however, can best be described by the term used by one of their own number, "Glittering Misery."

Regardless of the salutary effect their presence had upon their husbands, army wives, according to the *Army Regulations,* enjoyed the status of camp followers. The dauntless Elizabeth B. Custer somewhat petulantly observed that, in spite of the great value placed in the presence of an officer's wife with him on the frontier, the *Regulations* ignored wives entirely. She reported that the *Regulations,* nevertheless, entered into the minutest details concerning such prosaic matters as how long bean soup should be boiled. Even servants and company laundresses rated mention, and the army provided the laundresses with quarters, a daily ration, and the services of the post surgeon. The only heading, however, which could be interpreted to cover army dependents was the rule concerning the status of "camp followers." Mrs. Custer also related that the commanding officer of a post had complete control over the camp followers and could detain or ban them from post as he chose.[5]

The first problem confronting a newly-married officer's lady concerned the means of transportation to the far-off army post. In the late 1860s and early 1870s, with the trans-continental railroads not yet completed, women traveled by train as far as the railhead. There they transferred to stagecoaches for the remaining journey. On her first trip West in 1871, Frances Roe, wife of Second Lieutenant Fayette Roe, traveled from Kit Carson to Fort Lyon, Colorado Territory, in a "funny looking" stage-coach, called a "jerkey," which "seesawed back and forth and then sideways in an awful breakneck way."[6] Usually husbands met their wives at the stage depot nearest the post, and they then drove the final miles in army ambulances or Doughtery wagons that the officers borrowed.

In 1874, Katherine Garrett, soon to become the bride of Lieutenant Francis Gibson of the 7th Cavalry, traveled by train from Washington, D.C., to the railhead in Columbia, Dakota Territory, where her sister and brother-in-law, Mollie and Lieutenant Donald McIntosh, met her. Excitement had filled Kate Garrett's trip westward. She, quite mistakenly, appropriated Monsieur Jean Baptiste Bois's trousers, indulged too freely in firewater, and befriended a notorious stage robber, Doc Wilson.[7] Needless to say, Katherine Garrett, with her penchant for adventure, added to the color exhibited by those who formed the inner circle of General George A. Custer's command stationed at Fort Abraham Lincoln, Dakota Territory.[8]

Other women such as Emily McCorkle FitzGerald reached the Pacific Coast in 1874 by sailing down the Atlantic coastline, crossing the Isthmus of Panama by rail, and then sailing up the Pacific Coast until they reached their destination. Mrs. FitzGerald, four-months pregnant and seasick, summed up her feelings in a letter to her sister. "I am so tired of the water I hope to live the next four years out of sight of it entirely." Emily FitzGerald, then in San Francisco, still faced a sea voyage through the Inland Passage to Sitka, Alaska Territory.[9]

Husbands sometimes took extra measures to make traveling more comfortable for their wives. General Custer wrote to his father-in-law in July, 1865, that he had a spring wagon outfitted for Mrs. Custer, "so fixed that she can lie down in it, curtained, fitted up as a dressing room with adjustable seats, india-rubber roof, rain proof."[10] In September, 1877, while enroute to Camp Baker, Montana Territory, Lieutenant Roe had an army wagon rigged up immigrant-style and padded with canvas and straw on the sides and floor. He also folded their tent into a camp seat on which Mrs. Roe could sit and talk to the mules pulling the wagon behind them.[11]

Perhaps the most harrowing journey undertaken in army transportation occurred during the winter flight of Colonel Henry B. Carrington's command as it retreated from Fort Phil Kearney to Fort McPherson in Janaury, 1867. Colonel Carrington, held responsible for the Fetterman "Massacre," was ordered back to Fort McPherson. The command, including Frances Grummond, newly widowed and six-months pregnant, departed from Fort Phil Kearney on January 23, 1867, during a raging blizzard. The weather turned so cold that the mercury congealed in the thermometer at -40°F. On the morning of January twenty-fifth, the men refused to rise when reveille sounded, and the colonel had to order soldiers to lash their legs with whips in order to start their circulation and bring them to their feet. The most perilous part of the trip came during the ascent of a bluff which rose nearly sixty feet above the Crazy Woman Fork of the Powder River. The soldiers had to double-team each wagon, and then they pushed and pulled each wagon up the steep incline. Frances Grummond, unable to offer any assistance, remained inside and clung for dear life to the side of the wagon. After a seemingly impossible trek, the bedraggled command pulled into the entrance of Fort Reno and safety. Frances Grummond returned home to Tennessee and a few weeks later gave birth to a son.[12]

Another officer's wife, also pregnant, endured a similar overland march in bitter winter weather. Mrs. Paddock, wife of Lieutenant Richard B. Paddock, accompanied the 6th Cavalry on its journey back from the Brulé-Sioux Campaign of 1890-91. On Janaury 30, 1891, they broke camp at 4:30 a.m. and marched all day during a severe snowstorm. That night they camped on the Belle Fourché River where they experienced difficulty in obtaining water from the almost solidly-frozen stream. Because of the bitter weather, Mrs. Paddock traveled in a Red Cross ambulance and reclined on blankets. When they bivouacked in the evening, the first chore undertaken by the soldiers was to pitch her tent and warm it quickly with a Sibley stove. Then the troops carefully carried Mrs. Paddock, blankets and all, into the warmed tent. On this overland trip to Fort McKinney, the temperature again dropped to a low of -40°F. Supposedly because of his pre-natal experiences, the son to whom Mrs. Paddock later gave birth exhibited unusual immunity to cold weather.[13]

The presence of a child or children complicated an overland crossing. Three little boys, Harry and Jimmy Carrington and Bobby Wands, traveled with the Carrington command on its long way back to Fort McPherson and suffered from the bitter cold. In order to carry their infants safely, Elizabeth Burt and Frances Boyd converted champagne baskets into travel-bassinets; and Martha Summerhayes laced her three-month-old Harry into an Apache papoose cradle. The trip from Camp Apache to Camp Verde, Arizona Territory, in April, 1875, almost cost young Harry's life. Because of the constant pitching and rolling of the ambulance, Mrs. Summerhayes could nurse her son only when the column stopped at noon or at night. The strong alkali water caused the infant to break out in blisters and running sores, especially on the back of his head. The baby also suffered when giant ants attacked him as he lay inside his family's tent. The soldiers setting up camp had inadvertently pitched the Summerhayes's tent over an immense ant hill.[14]

Army wives experienced numerous other hardships en route between stations besides caring for children, suffering from the caprices of nature, and enduring creature discomforts. Sometimes they had to face the threat of Indian attack; or, even worse, they came under fire. Lieutenant A.H. Wands journeying from Fort

Mrs. Julia Gill Schnyder, second wife of Ordnance Sergeant Leodegar Schnyder. Because of her physical defect, she was known as "crosseyed-Julia." According to John D. McDermott, she probably worked as a company laundress at the time of her marriage in 1864. Courtesy Fort Laramie National Historic Site, Fort Laramie, Wyoming.

Mrs. William Pratt around 1884. Mrs. Pratt was the wife of a private in Company C, 7th Infantry. They were stationed at Fort Laramie until March 1890 when the fort was abandoned. Courtesy Fort Laramie National Historic Site, Fort Laramie, Wyoming.

Mrs. Brant C. Hammond, wife of Chaplain Hammond, in her parlor at Fort Sill, circa 1900. Courtesy U.S. Army Field Artillery & Fort Sill Museum, Fort Sill, Oklahoma.

Mrs. Tonamichel, wife of a Hospital
Steward at Fort Laramie in the 1880's
and mother of Jake Tonamichel.
Courtesy of Fort Laramie National
Historic Site, Fort Laramie,
Wyoming.

Officers' wives helping distribute supplies to Indians at Camp Supply, Indian Territory,
circa 1871. Courtesy National Archives.

Reno to Fort Carrington (later Fort Phil Kearney) on June 20, 1866, led a complement of twenty-six, including two women — one his own wife. The detachment was attacked by the Sioux at Crazy Woman's Fork, and the situation appeared extremely desperate. After half of the men had been wounded, they and the rest of the command decided that if the Indians overran their position they would kill themselves and the two women rather than face the tortures of Red Cloud's Sioux. Only the arrival of Captain Thomas B. Burrowes and two hundred men of the 18th Infantry saved the detail. One of the participants in the battle wrote that throughout the ordeal the two women "acted as angels of mercy and tenderness and looked after the wounded most heroically."[15]

The next year, on November 13, 1867, Major Andrew S. Burt's wagon train en route to Fort Phil Kearney was attacked at Crazy Woman's Fork. The Indians, striving to drive off the command's mules, were quickly repulsed. During the skirmish Mrs. Burt, her sister Kate, Christina, a Mormon hired girl, and the Burts' two children lay flat on the mattress inside an army ambulance. Afterwards, Major Burt asked his wife how she liked the Indian war whoops. Shedding tears of thankfulness and relief, Mrs. Burt replied, "God grant I may never hear another."[16]

Martha Summerhayes endured the taxing psychological strain of a seemingly imminent Indian attack during the harrowing journey through Sanford Pass, Arizona Territory, in April, 1875. Acting according to instructions, she lay down in the bottom of the ambulance, took out and cocked her derringer. Her husband had warned her that if he were wounded and the situation appeared hopeless, then she must kill their baby and herself. "Don't let them get either of you alive." Luckily, they made it through the pass without incident, and Jack Summerhayes relieved his tensions in an uncharacteristic manner by calling to his wife: "See the river yonder? We'll cross that tonight and then we'll be out of their God dammed country." Ella Baily and her baby, riding in the ambulance behind the Summerhayes' vehicle, had endured the same uncertainty.[17]

Although very few army women actually were attacked by Indians, they knew that they were not to be taken alive. During the most trying day at Fort Phil Kearney, while the command was out retrieving the bodies of the dead, the troops at the fort had orders that if the Indians overran the post, the women and children were to be put in the powder magazine and destroyed "all together, rather than have any captured alive."[18] Elizabeth Custer viewed her danger from the Indians as twofold because she "was in peril from death or capture by the savages, and liable to be killed by my own friends to prevent my capture."[19] Mrs. Sarah E. Canfield endured an Indian assault while stationed at Camp Cook, Montana Territory, in May, 1868. Fearing that the 2500 Indians would overrun the fort, the four women present decided that they would rather be shot by their own men than be taken captives by the Indians. As happened in many instances, however, the hostiles chose to retreat from the heavy artillery and infantry fire rather than storm the walls. Saved from destruction, one of the ladies, Mrs. William Auman, gave birth prematurely to a daughter the next day.[20]

Exposure to the elements was another hazard faced by women while journeying between stations. Katherine Garrett and he sister Mollie McIntosh spent one miserable night trapped in an army ambulance with a deranged soldier who was being transported to Bismarck, Dakota Territory. A violent thunder and hail storm arose, and the thunder and lightning caused the mules to bolt and run away. After an unpleasant night, during which Mollie comforted the insane man by pretending to be his sister, they were rescued by Elizabeth Custer, the doctor, and a few others who became alarmed when the mules returned to post alone.[21]

Perhaps the most desperate situation endured by army dependents occurred when they became lost during a sudden blizzard. Mrs. Elizabeth Burt and her friends, lost in an army ambulance and warmed by two buffalo robes, survived overnight exposure to a raging snowstorm. In October, 1866, Mrs. Burt and her sister accepted an invitation to visit Major and Mrs. John McClintock at Camp Douglas, Utah Territory. After a pleasant sojourn, the callers started back to Fort Bridger. En route home they became lost in the rapidly falling snow which quickly obscured landmarks and made further travel impossible. The women conferred with Mason, their driver, and decided to stop, spend the night, and hope that by morning the storm would abate. The next day the heavy snowfall continued making travel still infeasible. Their situation appeared hopeless until late that afternoon when a wood detail returning to Fort Bridger discovered them and informed the party that they had spent a miserable twenty-four hours within a quarter-mile of home.[22]

Officers' wives also coped with insects and reptiles during their treks between stations. Elizabeth Custer, during the march overland between Yankton and Fort Rice, Dakota Territory, counted more rattlesnakes than she had seen in five years in Texas and Kansas. When the column camped at night, the enlisted men systematically cut away the underbrush and beat the ground in order to kill or drive out all the snakes. Mrs. Custer wrote that the soldiers killed as many as forty rattlesnakes in one evening. Elizabeth also recalled that while they were stationed in Texas, General Custer "shook and beat" all her clothes in search of scorpions as he helped her dress. A centipede bit Eliza, the Custers' black maid. The insect, according to Eliza "crept into my bedclothes and got a good chance at me, I can tell you." The company surgeon treated the insect bite by giving Eliza a healthy drink of whiskey. Martha Summerhayes reported that she always felt more secure while tenting on the plains if her bed were encircled by a horsehair lariat.[23]

Once an officer's wife arrived on post, her initial priority concerned the selection of quarters. Quarters, as many other phases of army life, hinged on rank and seniority. A second lieutenant stood at the bottom of the hierarchy, and every officer his senior in rank and length of service took precedence. When an officer with higher rank or seniority arrived on post, the "ranking out" process began. One officer's wife called the procedure "bricks falling" because the new arrival had his choice of all the quarters occupied by his junior officers. Once he had chosen, the officer occupying those quarters had to move immediately. He, in turn, chose the unit occupied by one of his junior officers, and so the process continued down the line. At Fort Clark, Texas, a captain forced Lieutenant and Mrs. Oremus B. Boyd to move out even though Mrs. Boyd was still suffering from childbed fever and two of her three children had whooping cough. The Boyds, five in number, then occupied quarters consisting of one room and a detached kitchen. Mrs. Boyd, nevertheless, considered herself more fortunate than a young bride who, a few years previously at the same post, had been ranked out of quarters and then set up housekeeping in a hallway. Her young husband resigned when a senior officer chose their hall.[24]

Frances Roe never quite forgave Captain Park who, on extremely short notice, ranked them out. The senior officer, taken by the charm of the Roes' newly furnished home, decided to pull rank. Rather incensed, Mrs. Roe stated: "And that means we have been driven out of our house and home, bag and baggage because a captain wanted that one set of quarters!" She further related

Lt. Colonel Melville A. Cochran, 5th Infantry, and his family in front of their quarters at Fort Davis in 1889. Mrs. Cochran wrote *Posie; or From Reveille to Retreat*. Courtesy Fort Davis National Historic Site, Fort Davis, Texas.

Captain Jack Crawford's Quarters, Fort Craig, New Mexico Territory, circa 1880's. Courtesy Collections in the Museum of New Mexico, Santa Fé, New Mexico.

Quarters of Mr. and Mrs. Joe Nevins at Fort Union, New Mexico Territory, circa 1886. Nevins either served as a trumpeter or a tailor. Courtesy Fort Davis National Historic Site, Fort Davis, Texas.

that she had received a note at ten in the morning requesting that they vacate by one o'clock that afternoon. Frances Roe observed that she felt like a poor woman evicted for nonpayment of rent. To make an unpleasant situation worse, General Phillips [William Penrose], second in command at Camp Supply, ordered Findlay, their striker, back to his company as a cook. Findlay spent one day in the company kitchen before the general transferred him to his own. The quarters that the Roes finally occupied consisted of two rooms with a detached kitchen, newly converted from a chicken house.[25]

The quality of housing available at any given frontier post depended on the interrelation of numerous factors, including the date of establishment of the post, availability of suitable building materials, location in relation to the railroads or supply routes, and the presence or absence of hostiles in the vicinity. Two reports published by the Surgeon General's Office, *Circular Number 4, A Report of Barracks and Hospitals with Descriptions of Military Posts, 1870,* and *Circular Number 8, A Report of the Hygiene of the United States Army with Descriptions of Military Posts, 1875,* described the frontier posts then in existence and outlined the condition of housing available on each post.

Army wives, however, summed up living conditions on the frontier posts in much more vivid terms than did either of these official reports. Mrs. Burt recalled that in 1867 the commanding officer of Fort Fetterman, General Henry W. Wessels, lived in a dugout. During an early assignment on the frontier, Frances Boyd lived in a doubled tent for two years at Camp Halleck, Nevada. Since the winters were cold, a large stove occupied most of the outer tent, and the Boyds constructed a fireplace in the inner one. A double bed filled the rest of the available space in the inner tent and made the process of warming oneself extremely difficult. The Boyds also faced the problem of keeping the tents warm enough without burning them down.[26]

According to *Circular Number 4,* officers' quarters at Camp Verde, Arizona Territory, in 1870, consisted of "miserable hovels"; the commanding officer's quarters were constructed from "rough boards with gaping seams." In 1871, long, low adobe buildings comprised the quarters occupied by officers at Fort Lyon, Colorado Territory. Heavy wooden shutters, for protection during sand and snow storms, covered the windows. A ditch called an *acequia* ran through the post and brought water for the shade trees and lawns. Lieutenant and Mrs. Roe lived in newly-built quarters at Fort Lyon. Their home included a hall, stairway, and three rooms on the first floor, two rooms and a large closet on the second floor, and a detached kitchen — in all, much more generous housing than usually allotted to a second lieutenant.[27]

The quality of the quarters assigned to the Roes the next year at Camp Supply, Indian Territory, had not been improved since an entry in the *Medical History, 1869,* reported that both officers and enlisted men's quarters had earthen floors that were so damp that toadstools and mushrooms sprang up overnight and had to be cut down each morning. Frances Roe added that the walls of the quarters had been constructed from cottonwood logs which warped as the wood dried out and became infested with an army of bugs which plagued the residents at night.[28] Elizabeth Custer described typical army quarters as "severely plain with plastered walls, wood-work . . . once painted . . . usually disfigured by huge stoves." She further observed that "it was hard to give a cosey, home-like look to a sitting room without blinds, with plastered walls and without an open fire."[29]

In July, 1866, Andrew and Elizabeth Burt arrived at Fort Bridger, Wyoming Territory. Mrs. Burt discovered that the quartermaster had no cleaning supplies such as paint, calcimine, or white-wash available. She and Maggie, the cook, tried to clean the quarters as best they could. The Burts' residence consisted of four plastered rooms, two rooms on each side of a wide hall. All four rooms contained fireplaces, and the kitchen came equipped with an old cookstove held together by wires. Mrs. Burt had brought along a Brussels carpet with which she covered the living room floor. She fashioned coverings for the other floors from army blankets sewn together. The former residents had left behind beds, a few tables, and some chairs. To enliven the otherwise drab surroundings, Elizabeth made colorful curtains and covered the packing boxes that served as washstands and toilet tables with the same bright material. Since the quartermaster had no kerosene available, the Burts utilized candles for lighting.[30]

Sometimes the post quartermaster proved a difficult adversary for army wives intent upon gaining supplies. Frances Roe described the quartermaster at Camp Supply, in 1872, as "most arrogant," a man who "seems to think that every nail and tack is his own personal property and for his exclusive use." Elizabeth Custer once encountered the same type of quartermaster as did Frances Roe. His own quarters were equipped with the latest conveniences and the house kept in a first-rate state of repair.

Frances M.A. Roe and her dog Hal. Mrs. Roe's joyous *Army Letters from an Officer's Wife* is one of the most vivid and accurate accounts written by an officer's wife.

Consequently, all the other officers' wives grew envious of his fortunate spouse. Mrs. Custer reported that the covetous supply officer received a measure of justice when he was aroused from his warm bed one Christmas morning by a "dishevelled tipsy Jezebel of a camp woman" ringing his doorbell. [No one else had a doorbell.] Bracing herself against the door facing, the woman delivered this cryptic statement: "It's cold and my nose bleeds." On later occasions, the officers' wives summed up bad days or unhappy events with "It's cold and my nose bleeds."[31]

Once an officer's lady secured quarters, the question of reliable servants arose. The most trustworthy and available servant on the frontier army post was the striker, or, as his fellow soldiers contemptuously called him, the "dog robber." The striker, an enlisted man, worked for the officer during his off-duty hours and received from five to ten dollars a month, depending on the type and amount of work he performed.[32] Some strikers such as "Bowen the Immortal" became famous in the memoirs of their mistresses. Martha Summerhayes vowed that she could not have survived her life on the frontier without the faithful ministrations of Charles Bowen. While stationed at Ehrenberg, Arizona Territory, in 1875, Mrs. Summerhayes also employed a Cocopah Indian named Charlie as a butler-valet. Charlie "understood how to open a bottle of Cocomonga [Caucamonga wine] gracefully, and pour it as well," although his characteristic state of undress shocked what few guests the Summerhayes entertained at remote Ehrenberg.[33]

The chores undertaken by the striker depended on his various talents and attachment to the family. Mrs. Custer somewhat romanticized the striker whom she saw "as too devoted to the wife of his company officer to see her do anything." Elizabeth believed that the soldier-striker "had a special fondness for children and knew how to amuse them." According to Mrs. Custer, "the strikers' willing hearts made them quick to learn all kinds of domestic work." Frances Boyd employed a striker so devoted to her that he even did the laundry, even though he had to endure the ridicule of his fellow soldiers for undertaking that chore. The Roes hired several good men including Findlay, whom a senior officer appropriated, and Farrar whose most outstanding characteristic was that he liked Hal, the Roes' pet greyhound.[34]

Immediately after the Civil War while several of the regiments were stationed on police duty in the South, blacks enlisted in the army and became regular fixtures in some officers' households.

Mrs. Custer remarked that "Army people like the Negroes and find a quality of devotion in them that is most grateful when one is so dependent on servants as everyone is in military life." Frances Roe, while residing at Camp Supply in 1872, observed that one advantage of being located at a post occupied by black soldiers was that "one can always have good servants." Mrs. Vincent, also residing at Camp Supply at that time, employed two black enlisted men; one served as a cook, and the other, as the family butler. At Fort Sill, about 1881, the Henry family hired Gibson, a young black soldier, who acted as young Guy's nursemaid-companion.[35]

As with other good things in army life, General Orders No. 92 of 1870 outlawed the army striker by stating that "it shall be unlawful for any officer to use any enlisted man as a servant in any case whatever."[36] This General Order was not and still is not enforced or enforceable. Testifying before the Banning Committee on Reorganization of the Army in 1876, Colonel Robert E. Johnston asserted that if inspectors "make a very thorough investigation they will find that there are very few officers on the frontier who would not be brought to trial by court-martial for that offense. . . ." Colonel Johnston further remarked that at "one time or another, nearly all officers had been compelled to use enlisted men as servants." Captain Guy V. Henry, Sr., appearing before the same committee, justified his use of enlisted men as strikers by stating: "The prices we have to pay for servants are very high — from $25 to $30 per month is the usual price. That taken from the officers' pay would reduce it materially."[37]

In addition to strikers, officers and their families employed governesses, housemaids, cooks, and male servants who worked as butlers, valets, and cooks. The most famous couple who served on the frontier were, without doubt, Eliza and Henry, the Custers' Negro servants. The duo finally broke up when Henry married Manda, Mrs. B.C. Card's nursemaid. Eliza later married one of her many suitors and was replaced in the Custers' household by Mary Adams.[38]

Female servants, rarities on the frontier, proved as hard to keep as to obtain. At first, the officers' wives wanted attractive servants; but soon they found that pretty maids became enamored of their own good looks and popularity and refused to work or resigned and got married. Elizabeth Custer reported that the wife of Fort Sully's commander had employed four governesses and all of them had married other officers and resigned. The lady, more realistically, then hoped to employ an "antiquated and old

30

An enlisted "Striker" and his charges at Fort Shaw, Montana in 1889. Courtesy U.S. Signal Corps, National Archives.

governess."[39]

During the summer of 1866, Frances Carrington, stationed at Fort Laramie, hired an Indian woman to do the laundry. In her industrious attempt to remove stains, she rubbed holes into the clothing. Lydia Spenser Lane recalled that she employed a cook while they lived at Fort Union, New Mexico Territory. Old Martin, as she described her, "ugly as she was," won the hand of a stone-mason at the fort almost immediately. Mrs. Lane hardly missed her services because Old Martin was uncomely, mean-tempered, and "to crown it all, a wretched cook." When Frances Boyd returned to the frontier from New York where her second child had been born, she brought back a servant whose appearance "was so far from pleasing, it seemed safe to take her." During the five months she graced the Boyds' household, the maid complained so much that Mrs. Boyd felt only relief when she departed. Grace Paulding, who also had problems with help, wrote that during the 1890s she engaged a maid who within two months had "collected such a train of admirers among the enlisted men that she had less and less time to give to the sordid details of cooking our meals and cleaning our house."[40]

Emily McCorkle FitzGerald filled her letters to her mother with complaints about her servants. Mary, a young black girl whom she took to Alaska with her, found the soldiers too attractive; and Jennie, an Alaskan Indian, developed a taste for whiskey. Finally, with great reluctance, Emily FitzGerald hired a Chinese houseboy. He, too, gave unsatisfactory service because he had the unpleasant habit of sprinkling the laundry by squirting it with mouthfuls of water. That repulsive habit was aggravated by the fact that his teeth were decayed.[41]

Frances Roe employed at least two Chinese servants. One, named Charlie, developed a strong attachment for her chickens. He often talked to them in Chinese and resented the striker's feeding them corn. In another episode, the Roes' houseboy, Hang, and their striker, Volmer, did not always work well together; and Mrs. Roe often had to intervene to keep the peace. Volmer had expressed his dislike for Hang when he first arrived by tying him down to the bed with a picket rope. Mrs. Roe, who rushed to her houseboy's aid, reported that "his eyes had turned green and he was frothing at the mouth." Another incident with racial overtones occurred when Sam, Mrs. Anson Mills's Chinese servant, committed suicide after he had won some money from a white soldier who accused him of cheating and threatened to kill him.[42]

32

Frances Roe recalled a more humorous incident involving a recalcitrant Chinese servant. An officer's wife at Camp Baker, Montana Territory, in 1877, employed a houseboy who would not follow her washing instructions. When she attempted to correct his method, the "heathen looked at her with a grin and said, 'Alee light, you no likee my washee, you washee yousel.' " With that ultimatum, he lifted the wash boiler off the stove and poured the entire contents on the floor.[43]

Army wives also faced the taxing problems created by the scarcity of certain foodstuffs on the frontier and the exorbitant expense of transporting such items to the remote regions of the West. Arriving at Fort C.F. Smith in the spring of 1868, two daring traders received fifteen dollars per bushel for potatoes and onions. In the early 1870s, Mrs. Ellen Biddle paid two dollars each for a dozen eggs and a pound of butter. She also reminisced that an officer at Fort Whipple, Arizona Territory, once paid seven dollars for a dozen oysters shipped in cracked ice from Baltimore.[44]

The women soon learned to adapt their recipes to the supplies at hand. Some of the ladies kept cows and chickens — when those domestic animals were allowed on post. Otherwise, they made apple pies without apples and custards without milk and eggs. Frances G. Carrington wrote that at Fort Phil Kearney in 1866, Mrs. William H. Bisbee concocted mince pies from beef hearts, dried apples, raisins, and sweetened vinegar. The Commissary Department in an attempt to provide a variety of food, stocked desiccated vegetables compacted into cakes. These received a poor reception because the cooked product remained tasteless. Mrs. Burt expressed the majority opinion when she remarked: "After one trial we never wished to add them to our larder."[45]

The ladies, just as their civilian counterparts, needed proper culinary tools and often found themselves having to improvise. If they arrived on the frontier without kitchenware, they could order them or obtain them at a post auction. The post quartermaster sometimes allowed the women to use company utensils; but an anecdote told by Martha Summerhayes demonstrates that this equipment often was less than serviceable. She tried to use army cooking tools, but she could not find anything smaller than "two-gallon tea kettles, yard-long meatforks, and mess-kettles deep enough to cook rations for fifty men." Her first efforts using the oversized pots and pans failed, and her husband greeted her tears with, "You are pampered and spoiled with your New

England kitchens." Jack Summerhayes told his wife that she must join in the spirit of life on the frontier. "You will have to learn to do as other army women do — cook in cans and such things, be inventive and learn to do with nothing."[46]

In addition to servants and household chores, children, quite expectedly, occupied a great part of the women's daily lives. Children on the frontier army posts added complications to their parents' lives; but, perhaps, the greatest problem children posed to their mothers was the discomforts of pregnancy and childbirth in less than ideal locations. Some army wives, not yet blessed with children, occupied their time by thinking and talking about babies; while those of their peers who had children probably spent their time avoiding their husbands in the evenings. Emily FitzGerald, at Fort Lapwai, Idaho Terrtiroy, in 1876, reported on the maternal status of the ladies on the post. Of the three other ladies present, none had children; and they, as she pointedly phrased it, "would give their heads to have a baby and are just as busily engaged trying all sorts of means so as to have one." Emily, mother of two, hoped she would not become pregnant again. Indeed, while she had been stationed at Sitka, she and the other ladies had "engaged in wondering how to prevent any more babies coming." A rather fanciful method of birth control adopted by Mrs. FitzGerald consisted of her preparing a complete layette for her third child because she reasoned that if she were ready for it, the baby would not arrive. Elizabeth Custer, because of the hardships and discomforts of frontier army life, grew to be thankful that she had remained childless.[47]

Mrs. FitzGerald had made extensive preparations in anticipation of her second child, Herbert, born October 30, 1874. She wrote her mother that she had gotten ready for her confinement by securing new gowns for herself, a complete layette for the baby, a collection of muslin rags, and all items necessary for the labor bed. In a passage remarkably frank for a woman writing in the Victorian Era, Mrs. FitzGerald described the birth of her son:

> . . . I did not suffer nearly so much as I did with Bess, though it was awfully bad anyway, but as soon as I had the first bearing down pains Docter [her husband] gave me chloroform and I did not feel another until the last one. Mama, it made it so much easier. I did not have any tired worn out feeling after the baby was born but felt as if I had had a comfortable sleep. I got sick

about ten in the evening, just as I did with Bess, and was awfully disappointed that it did not come more quickly than it did. Most everybody has a much shorter time with the second baby, but I suffered dreadfully from about eleven until four. . . .[48]

Quite often, because of the conditions under which babies were born and the medical practices of the day, women developed childbed fever as a complication of childbirth. Even with the strictest and most scientific care her doctor-husband could give her, Emily FitzGerald contracted acute peritoneal inflammation on the eleventh day of her confinement. More than thirty hours elapsed before she passed the crisis and began her recovery. During the first day of the illness while she suffered most, her husband kept her under the influence of chloroform for more than an hour.[49]

An indifferent, nurse, who seemed intent on murdering both mother and child, complicated Frances Boyd's recovery after the birth of her first child. Martha Summerhayes's recuperation after the birth of her son suffered from the inattention of a young army surgeon who appeared "much better versed in the sawing off of soldiers' legs than in the treatment of young mothers and babies." In June, 1877, while stationed at Fort Whipple, Ellen Biddle gave birth to a son whom they christened James Harwood. Both mother and child remained in delicate health, and the child survived only three weeks. Perhaps as a psychosomatic reaction to his death, Mrs. Biddle developed a mysterious eye ailment which resisted treatment for six weeks after the baby's death.[50]

Late in October, 1875, Emily FitzGerald miscarried, hemorrhaged and lost all her strength. She continued to nurse year-old Bert until a week later and then had to stop. Her husband treated her with cod liver oil, iron, and quinine. Emily wrote her mother that she was thankful that she would not have another "Sitka baby"; and in a second very frank remark she observed that: "I don't believe there is a safe day in the month for me. Indeed, I know there isn't — 15th — 16th — 17th — or any other." She also added that she and her two intimate friends, Mrs. Campbell and Mrs. Fields, "held meetings of horror" concerning birth control. Quite ruefully, she remarked: "We all seem to be awfully prolific."[51]

Babies did not show much consideration in the timing of their arrivals. Frances Boyd recalled that during one march overland between Arizona and Texas, nine babies were born. The command stopped twenty-four hours for each mother to recover before continuing the journey. Kate Gibson learned that her husband had once been called upon to deliver the baby of an enlisted man's wife who went into labor while en route to join her husband at his new station.[52]

As in the case of Ellen Biddle, the death of a child brought great heartache to parents and friends, and members of the army post rallied around the bereaved family and offered aid and sympathy. Kate Gibson remembered the death of Captain and Mrs. Federick Benteen's youngest child. Since no coffin could be obtained at Fort Rice, Dakota Territory, a soldier constructed a plain pine box which Mrs. Gibson lined with the silk and taffeta from her wedding dress. No clergyman was present to conduct the funeral so the mourners simply "walked to the little cemetery on the hill, knelt beside the small grave and commended the baby's soul to the Father whence it came." On a trip back East after the death of her son, Ellen Biddle stated: "I left with one long tender regret, for the grave of my little son under the shadow of the great mountain had to remain.[53]

Whether en route west in an army ambulance, by train or boat, tenting on the plains, or in her frontier home, the army wife waged a constant battle against the forces of nature. In January, 1872, at Fort Lyon, Frances Roe went riding with Lieutenants Alden and Baldwin. Quite suddenly, a sandstorm blew up on the surrounding plain, catching the riders outside the garrison. Just before the storm struck in full force, Lieutenant Baldwin took the reins of Frances's horse on the right and instructed Lieutenant Alden to ride close to her left side. Mrs. Roe described the wind as almost hurricane-force; and Lieutenant Baldwin warned her that whatever she did, she must sit tightly in her saddle and not jump. Being a woman given to quick impulses, Frances leaped off her horse, ran, and clung to the picket fence in front of the chaplain's house. When the storm had finally passed and the officer had gotten over his anger, Mrs. Roe observed that her face, pitted by the grains of sand, looked as if she had just recovered from smallpox. The storm occurred on a Monday and wreaked havoc with the family washes that departed for "regions unknown."[54]

At Cimarron Redoubt, Kansas, in January, 1873, Fayette and Frances Roe encountered their first "norther." The snow, driven by the fierce wind, sifted in between the logs of the inner walls and in around the windows, almost burying them. When the intensely cold morning came, the Roes' strikers had to sweep away the snow before they could start fires in the stoves. After the occupants of the Redoubt depleted the meager wood supply, soldiers had to go outside the fortifications to gather more. Meanwhile the Roes chinked the cracks in their walls with scraps of blankets and covered the dirt floor with clean grain bags.[55]

Nature provided a summer menace in the form of grasshoppers which scourged the plains during the 1870s and destroyed all vegetation in their path. Ellen Biddle recalled a grasshopper invasion which occurred one Sunday afternoon in 1875 while they were living at Fort Lyon. The sky became obscured as if a severe thunderstorm threatened, and a dark cloud of the whirling, buzzing insects descended to earth. They devoured everything in their path, from the vines trailing over the porches to the hundreds of unripe watermelons growing in the troops' gardens. When the insects left with the wind the next day, not a blade of grass could be seen on post. In a more amusing episode, Colonel Benjamin H. Grierson wrote his wife, Alice, about the uproar a grasshopper invasion had created at Fort Leavenworth:

> They [grasshoppers] were impolite and unceremonious enough to hop up, get up or in some way make their merry way up under the hoops and skirts of the ladies who were bold enough to promenade among them . . . should the grasshoppers remain here very long, I have no doubt but what some Yankee will invent some pattern for the relief of the ladies in the way of *solid drawers.*[56]

With summer came the threat of severe thunder and hail storms. Frances Roe related that a destructive thunder and hail storm struck Fort Ellis, Montana Territory, in July, 1884. After the downpour passed, the Roes measured eight inches of hail standing on the floor of their shed, and Frances stated that the stones were as large as hens' eggs. The rain and hail streamed through broken windows and flooded quarters. In all, the hailstones broke nine hundred windows on post and devastated the company gardens. Other victims of the storm's fury were the hundreds of gophers living in nearby burrows that were drowned or beaten to death. Mrs. Frances Boyd reminisced that rainstorms at Fort Bayard, New Mexico Territory, caused such severe flooding that the ladies opened both the back and front doors and allowed the flood waters to run through their quarters.[57]

Army wives adapted to nature as best they could. While at Camp McDowell, Arizona Territory, Martha Summerhayes wore loose, white dresses because of the extreme heat. She adopted the Mexican mode of existence. She took daily siestas and learned to smoke Mexican cigarettes. At Ehrenberg, Mrs. Summerhayes bathed each day in the muddy Colorado. Although her husband refused to allow her to cook and to dress as the local women did, she felt that she had made a healthy adjustment to the frontier. An earthquake, however, disrupted her sense of security, and she became obsessed with the fear that if she did not get away she could not survive. The distraught woman imagined that the spirits of the dead in the community graveyard were haunting her: She could hear them whispering, "You'll be with us soon, you'll be with us soon."[58]

Other dangers existed on the frontier army posts besides the complications of birth, sand and hail storms, floods, blizzards, insects, and reptiles. In a few instances personal attacks were made on officers' wives. Elizabeth Custer recalled an incident in which a Negro recruit on guard duty fired a shot at a group of ladies on a late evening stroll about the post. Frances Roe wrote that an ex-striker entered Mrs. Norton's home in an attempted robbery and succeeded in frightening the poor woman senseless. Of course, Kate Garrett Gibson, in another of her narrow escapes, was rescued from a would-be ravisher by her intrepid "Robin Hood of the Old West," Doc Wilson.[59]

An incident of a more serious nature occurred at Fort Davis, Texas, in the fall of 1872. Mrs. Kendall, wife of Lieutenant Frederic Kendall, shot and killed Corporal Daniel Talliforro of the 9th Cavalry as he attempted to climb in her bedroom window. Because the corporal was black, the incident developed racial overtones. The officers and their families assumed that his intentions had been rape rather than robbery, because that "was expected of Negroes." Elizabeth Custer also feared black soldiers "whose early days of soldiering were a reign of terror to us women in our lonely unprotected homes."[60]

When their husbands went out on campaign, army wives had to deal with the ordeal of parting. Elizabeth Burt related the heartbreak she felt when the moment of leavetaking came. Andrew and she said goodbye behind the closed doors of their quarters; and he went to his "duty" and she, back to her room to her "tears and prayers." Mrs. Burt chose a back room where she could drown out "The Girl I Left Behind Me," the tune traditionally played by the band as the companies marched out of the post. Even Elizabeth Custer, who probably accompanied her husband

The Custers tenting on the plains with other officers and ladies from Fort Abraham Lincoln, Dakota Territory, 1875. Mrs. Custer is seated in the center, the general is dressed in buckskin and standing to her immediate left. Courtesy U.S. Signal Corps, National Archives.

more often than did any other officer's wife, remained behind on occasion. She described how bereft she felt at such times:

> . . . It is infinitely worse to be left behind, a prey to all the horrors of imagining what may happen to one you love. You eat your heart slowly out with anxiety, and to endure such suspense is simply the hardest of all trials that come to the soldier's wife.[61]

With her husband away in Oregon on official business, Emily FitzGerald found herself in a most stressful situation. She blamed the government and the Indians for the precariousness of her existence and expressed herself vehemently on the subject. On May 5, 1877, she wrote to her mother and related her feelings about the impasse between Chief Joseph and General O.O. Howard. "Oh, how I hate them [Indians]. I wish they could be exterminated, but without bloodshed among our poor soldiers. General Howard is promenading the porch quoting scriptures. . . ." On May 11, 1877, she again vented her disgust with Congress which had refused to appropriate funds for the army. She observed that "if the government is worth anything at all, out of respect for itself, it should keep a respectable Army."[62]

After the military forced Joseph to resist, Mrs. FitzGerald became even more incensed with the governmental policy and exploded. "Oh, the government, I hate it! Much it respects and cares for the soldier who at a moment's notice leaves his family and sacrifices his life for some mistaken Indian policy." She summed up the plight of the Indian-Fighting Army when she observed that all the "soldiers got was no pay and abuse from the country they risked their lives to protect." In August, Mrs. FitzGerald wrote that for the last ten days she had been too wretched to write. Indeed, she had never been so unhappy in all her life because the "uncertainty of everything in the future and this not knowing or hearing anything is the hardest thing to bear I have ever gone through."[63]

The women at Fort Abraham Lincoln in June and July, 1876, had existed in the same state of apprehension. They tried to go about their usual routines and even attended the annual Fourth of July ball, unaware of the events of the twenty-fifth of June. For two days prior to word of the Battle of the Little Bighorn, a "fearful depression had hung over the fort." On the evening of the fifth of July, the officers' wives gathered at Mrs. Custer's quarters and tried to sing hymns. One of the women playing the piano struck the opening chords of "Nearer My God to Thee" and was told by the others that particular song was not appropriate. Having no heart for music, they said the "Our Father" and went home for another sleepless night.[64]

On the morning of July 6, 1876, Captain William S. McCaskey, Doctor Johnson V.D. Middleton, Lieutenant C.L. Gurley, and two of the doctor's assistants appeared at Mrs. Custer's back door. Elizabeth Custer, clad in her dressing gown, came down to receive them in the parlor. She and the members of her intimate circle learned of their widowhood together. In an act of desperation, Margaret Custer Calhoun, who lost three brothers, a nephew, and her husband, ran after Captain McCaskey pleading, "Is there no message for me?" Although the day was already extremely warm, Elizabeth Custer asked for a wrap and accompanied the officers as they notified the other officers' wives and the wives of the enlisted men about their husbands' fates. In all, twenty-six women at Fort Abraham Lincoln had been widowed on June 25, 1876.[65]

The women at Fort Rice also suffered because they had no way of knowing the fate of their men who formed part of Custer's command. Kate Gibson remembered that they spent the night of July 5, 1876, at Lieutenant Charles de Rudio's quarters where they lay silently on the floor and waited for word to come. At every distant sound they sprang up hoping that it might be a courier with messages. When the mail finally arrived the next day, the women could hardly bear reading the dates on the envelopes or opening the letters. Kate Gibson's husband, with Benteen and Reno, survived while her sister Mollie's husband, Lieutenant Donald McIntosh, perished with Custer.[66]

A wife endured great emotional stress when she could not give her husband a proper burial. Emily FitzGerald told how Mrs. Thellar whose husband had been killed in the campaign against Chief Joseph in June, 1877, agonized over the fact that two weeks had passed before a burial party could inter her husband. She kept repeating: "Oh, my poor Ned, lying there with his face blackening in the sun." Captain Simon Snyder met Mrs. James Porter, wife of one of the officers killed with Custer, on board the *E.H. Durfee* on her way back East. Snyder observed that Mrs. Porter, mother of two young children, bore up well under her affliction, although her face showed what she had been through.[67]

A widow, regardless of the circumstances of her husband's death, lost all claim to government housing and had to vacate the quarters as soon as possible. Elizabeth Custer, the widow of a general, could have stayed on, but she chose to leave Fort Abraham Lincoln quickly because she could not stand being just a name on a pension roll. Frances Roe told the story of Mrs. White who had just given birth to her fifth child and whose husband died soon thereafter. The widow had to give up her quarters as soon as she and the baby were strong enough to travel.[68]

Survivors of soldiers killed during the Indian Wars faced numerous financial difficulties because the government provided only a meager pension to Indian Wars widows and their minor children. Since the sum received was grossly insufficient, Congress in 1908 increased the amount paid a widow to twelve dollars a month. Later, in 1913, Congress raised the survivor's rate to twenty dollars per month. On March 4, 1917, the government authorized certain survivors of the Indian Campaigns from 1859 to 1891 or their widows to receive annuities based on the rates established in the Act of 1913.[69]

Not all tours in the West could be considered hardship duty. Some posts such as Benicia and Angel Island, the Presidio of San Francisco, and other installations on the Pacific Coast provided welcome respites from the harshness of the frontier outposts to those lucky enough to receive these assignments. Martha Summerhayes, one of the fortunate ones, described her first tour at Angel Island. "The flowers ran riot in our garden, fresh fruits and vegetables, fresh fish, and all the luxuries of that marvelous climate were brought to our door." In addition to the abundance of fresh foods, the entertainment provided by the commanding officer and his wife enjoyed an army-wide reputation. Mrs. Kautz, the colonel's lady, "held grand court . . . and receptions, military functions, lawn tennis, bright uniforms were the order of the day." Mrs. Kautz and Martha Summerhayes read the German classics, went to the German theater, and entertained Friedrich Haase, star of the Royal Theater of Berlin. Frau Haase confirmed Mrs. Summerhayes's feelings when she described Angel Island as a veritable paradise.[70]

Life for an officer's wife on the frontier, complicated by all the various difficulties, nevertheless, was ameliorated by numerous social, recreational, and religious opportunities. Ellen Biddle described the fullness of her daily life at Fort Whipple. In the morning she usually rode or went driving, and she spent part of each day sewing because she made all of the children's and her own clothes. At that time Fort Whipple had the reputation of

42

being a very gay post with some kind of entertainment almost every evening. During this period when General August V. Kautz commanded the post, they had dinners, dances, and rehearsed the plays staged by the dramatic society. Mrs. Biddle happily recalled that time as the "days of the Empire."[71]

In October, 1878, Frances Roe wrote that garrison life at Fort Shaw became delightful in the winter after all the companies had returned from the long hard summer campaigns. The days of "wining and dining" began with the exchange of social courtesies. Almost daily some officer and his lady gave a dinner or card party. The dinners usually were "quite elegant, formal affairs, beautifully served with dainty china and handsome silver." Officers attended the socials in their full-dress uniforms which added to the glitter of the good life as celebrated on a frontier army post.[72]

In a most amusing letter, Mrs. Roe described a masked ball she attended in Helena while stationed at Camp Baker in February, 1878. Frances, who had not come prepared to attend a masquerade ball, quite ingeniously made a costume that thoroughly disguised her as a "Country Girl." Colonel Fitz-James [Floyd-Jones], the regimental colonel, paid Mrs. Roe the most flagrant courtesies. She kept insisting that he had mistaken her identity. The colonel just as insistently assured her that he knew her identity and persisted with his unwelcomed attentions. Mrs. Roe, quite disgusted with his suit, decided to reciprocate in the flirtation and led the officer a "dance." The poor colonel was speechless when his unmasked "Country Girl" revealed herself as Mrs. Fayette Roe, the wife of one of his lieutenants. The true object of his affections, a girl from Helena, had watched his performance in silence and with the same apparent irritation as had Fayette Roe.[73]

Mary R. Heistand, wife of Second Lieutenant Henry O. Heistand, gave one of the most unusual entertainments on the military frontier. Her banquet occurred during the holiday season of 1880-1881, when the Indians at Fort Peck's Poplar River Agency threatened an uprising. Previously, the army had dispatched two companies of the 11th Infantry from Fort Custer with orders to contain the situation. By December 16, 1880, the command had built rough, temporary quarters. The Heistands occupied two rooms, each about thirteen feet by seventeen and one-half feet.

Nine troops of mounted infantry and two troops of cavalry from Fort Keogh, and one troop of cavalry and a detachment of infantry from Fort Buford arrived in time to celebrate Christmas.

Family and servants pose in front of their quarters on Funston Avenue, the Presidio of San Francisco, circa 1880. Courtesy National Archives.

Children playing on Funston Avenue, the Presidio of San Francisco, circa 1880. Courtesy National Archives.

A lady strolling her infant in front of the Station Hospital at the Presidio of San Francisco, circa 1867. Courtesy the Bancroft Library.

Mrs. Heistand decided that she would invite some of the new-comers to a holiday dinner. The ten guests entered a room furnished with lace curtains, a hanging lamp, a piano newly arrived from Fort Custer, and carpeted with warm buffalo robes. Several potted geranium plants added a note of cheer to the surroundings.

Mrs. Heistand's dinner could just as easily been served in the best restaurants back East. The entrée, raw oysters, was served in individual cups carved from ice. The menu included:

> . . . home made soup, salmon croquettes with egg sauce and potatoes, sweet-breads served in patties with canned peas, roast beef, potatoes and cabbage à la cauliflower, prairie chicken and currant jelly tarts, canned asparagus salad, cheese and crackers, sherbet, homemade cake, and candies.

The diners remained three and one-half hours over the repast. All during the festivities, though, one thought remained in everyone's mind. If the Indian outbreak did come to pass, this could very well be their last meal.[74]

In more peaceful situations, army wives enjoyed socializing while they did their daily tasks. The sewing bee enabled the officers' ladies to get together, exchange news, work to complete a group project, or else just do the weekly mending. The ladies stationed at Fort Abraham Lincoln in the summer of 1874 joined forces and produced Kate Garrett's wedding gown and trousseau. Elizabeth Custer recalled that the women once made a complete wardrobe for two young children who desperately needed winter clothing. The ladies pored over *Godey's Lady's Book* and *Harper's Bazaar* for new ideas on clothing; and when Butterick patterns became available, the wives quickly adopted them in their attempt to keep up with the fashions back East.[75]

An officer's lady could find numerous other chores to occupy her time if she chose to take over some of the duties usually performed by the household servants. Frances Roe once incurred the wrath of her Chinese houseboy by making the bread. Ellen Biddle churned the milk, molded the butter, and also set the yeast dough. Mrs. Frances Boyd recalled the story of one young bride living at a desert post who stayed busy keeping the milk cool.[76]

Army women often enjoyed quiet evenings at home with reading, games, music, or quadrilles. In June, 1866, the officers and their ladies stationed at Fort Phil Kearney participated in "all-round social dancing, games of cards, and the authors game."

At Fort Shaw, in 1879, Fayette and Frances Roe, and their friends attended germans, luncheons, dinners, and card parties. In addition to staging tableaux, and operatic pantomimes, the Roes established a tradition when they gave the first cotillion in their regiment. Mrs. Emily FitzGerald also gave whist parties for her husband while they resided at Fort Lapwai in 1876. Officers' wives engaged in such daytime and seasonal sports as ice skating, sleigh riding, lawn tennis, croquet, and bowling.[77]

The ladies soon discovered that horseback riding was the most popular form of recreation available on the frontier. Women learned to ride almost as soon as they reached the western posts. Kate Garrett recalled that the first two questions every officer asked her were: "Do you ride? Do you shoot?" Mrs. Frances Boyd found horseback riding the "chief charm of Army life." Elizabeth Custer spent much of her time in the saddle and constantly had to reinforce the seams of her well-worn habit. Parting with her horse caused Frances Roe her greatest distress when they were transferred back East. Mrs. Roe enjoyed riding tremendously and wrote that "since I have been with the Army I have ridden twenty-two horses that have never been ridden by a woman before! . . . I was never unseated — not once!"[78]

Although Elizabeth Custer stated that she never mastered a firearm, army wives most generally learned to shoot simultaneously with learning to ride. Ellen Biddle reported an instance in which she and Mrs. C.C. Cresson had to be left alone in camp while the soldiers chased an escaped thief. The two women got their rifles ready and knew how to use them because they had attended target practice. Frances Roe often accompanied her husband when he hunted prairie chickens and ruffed grouse. Kate Garrett participated in a buffalo hunt and earned the distinction of being one of the few army women who killed a buffalo.[79]

Several of the ladies enjoyed fishing as a form of recreation in addition to the chance of a welcome change in the menu. On numerous occasions, Mrs. Frances Boyd caught enough fish for their evening meal at Camp Halleck, Nevada. Frances Roe, who excelled in all sports, became a champion angler although once her courage deserted her. One evening at Fish Lake near the Piegan Agency, Montana Territory, she grew frightened by the depth of the lake and had to be rowed back to shore. On a later outing, a Mrs. Ord from Omaha, General Stanley [T.H. Stanton], and Mrs. Roe enjoyed an outing in which the ladies caught 120

A masked ball of officers and their friends at Fort Sill, Indian Territory, 1897. Courtesy U.S. Signal Corps, National Archives.

Niece and daughters of Commissary Sergeant Thomas Forsyth along with male companions at Fort Davis, circa late 1880's. Young ladies are, left to right: Beulah Ralhouse, Mary Elizabeth and Clara Forsyth. Courtesy Fort Davis National Historic Site, Fort Davis, Texas.

Skating was one of the winter recreations enjoyed by army officers and their families at Fort Keogh in the late 1880's. Courtesy U.S. Signal Corps, National Archives.

Picnic on creek near Hartville, Wyoming, 1889. Left to right: 1st Lieutenant L.D. Greene, 7th Infantry, Mrs. Mary Buckley, Louis Brechemin, Jr., and his mother. Courtesy Fort Laramie National Historic Site, Fort Laramie, Wyoming.

Officers and ladies from Fort Huachuca picnicking in 1898. Courtesy Fort Huachuca Museum, Fort Huachuca, Arizona.

mountain trout.[80]

Music and theater provided another source of entertainment for the frontier army family. Kate Garrett and Mollie McIntosh sang and played their guitars. At Fort Abraham Lincoln, the Custers entertained their friends many evenings at home by gathering around the piano and singing favorite songs. Early in the 1870s, the officers and ladies at Fort D.A. Russell produced such plays as "Caste," "Lend Me Five Shillings," and "Faint Heart Never Won Fair Lady." While stationed at Fort Laramie, Major Andrew Burt starred in "Everybody's Friend," and "Camille." Frances Boyd recalled that while they were stationed at Fort Clark, Texas, her husband was acclaimed for his portrayal of "Old Eccles," a drunken reprobate, in "Caste." At Fort Clark, proceeds from their plays went to charity or were used to renovate the main hall in the garrison which served as a church, schoolroom, ballroom, and theater.[81]

Religion provided another important social outlet in addition to its spiritual consolation. Margaret Carrington described the usual Sunday Service at Fort Phil Kearney during the dark days of 1866. They sang praises to God and implored His divine help in their plight. A string band accompanied the worshippers as they sang "Magnificat," "Gloria in Excelsis," and "Old Hundred." Martha Summerhayes, however, wrote that while stationed at Old Camp McDowell, a remote post, she heard only one sermon, delivered by a Mormon bishop. She characterized his message as being "of a rather preposterous nature, neither instructive or edifying." At Fort Bidwell, California, in 1884, Reynolds Burt reminisced that the religious event of the year occurred when the Episcopal bishop came to conduct services. Both Elizabeth Burt and Emily FitzGerald organized Sunday School classes for the children at their posts.[82]

The army did not station chaplains at every post. Fort Union, one of the garrisons served by a chaplain, built up a thriving religious community during the 1880s. A member of the garrison band played the organ at church services; but, in the years before the congregation could afford an organ, the worshippers used various other instruments for accompaniment. During the 1860s Mrs. Lydia Spenser accompanied these services on her melodeon.[83]

The commanding officer at Fort Shaw in 1885 entrusted Frances Roe with the musical arrangements for Sunday Services. She selected six bandsmen for accompanists and a choir of four enlisted men. Mrs. Roe sat in the middle of the ten musicians and singers and directed them. Although Sergeant Moore, the tenor, sang in public, he refused to sing solo in church so Mrs. Roe "had to hum along for his ears alone."[84]

Officers' ladies traveled westward with their husbands out of love, a sense of duty, and the need to be where they felt most appreciated. As Frances Roe saw their function:

> We will see that the tents are made comfortable and
> cheerful at every camp, that the little dinner after the
> weary march, the early breakfast and the cold luncheon
> one and all are as dainty as camp cooking will permit.[85]

They endured the hardships and shared the panoply and joys of the dress parades and the forms of recreation they devised to pass their time. If they sometimes seemed a "little silly over brass buttons," they, nevertheless, agreed with Martha Summerhayes that they had married soldiers and where the federal government chose to send their men, they also would go.

The officers' wives faced the numerous hardships attendant with life upon an unsettled frontier; but, because of their social status and financial standing, they could afford the servants and facilities that made their lives more bearable. Other women, whose lives included more the miseries of frontier existence and fewer of the ameliorations, followed the Indian-Fighting Army westward.

3

ENLISTED MEN'S WIVES, LAUNDRESSES, AND CAMP FOLLOWERS"
"Who calmed each death with tears and prayer? 'Twas Comp'ny 'Haybag' 'Mag' O'Hare."

S E. Whitman wrote that women living on the frontier army posts fell into three categories: the wives and daughters of officers, wives and daughters of enlisted men, and the company laundresses.[2] 'Three other groups of women lived on or near the military reservations: the female servants of the officers' families and the wives and daughters of civilian employees, the Indian women, and the true "camp followers." Of all these women, only the laundresses were recognized by the army and given legal status. The army included all the others in the broadly-defined category of "camp followers" and put them under the direct supervision of the post commanders. While information about the other women on the military frontier remains fragmentary, they made contributions no less significant than those of the officers' ladies.

As a general rule, the United States Army kept no statistics on the number of married enlisted men. In fact, from the 1860s until at least World War I, the official governmental policy consisted of refusing to enlist married men and of discouraging soldiers from marriage. While the War Department never directly forbade enlisted men to marry, the bureaucracy made life for married soldiers as difficult and unappealing as possible.

In a series of General Orders and changes in the *Regulations*, dating from 1861 to 1910, the War Department kept narrowing the privileges granted to married enlisted men. General Orders No. 140 of 1861 stated that, although married enlisted men were not excluded from the army, their number in regimental service must be governed by the need for laundresses in the companies and in the general service, by the superintendents.[3] The *Revised Regulations, 1863* provided that no man having a wife or child could be enlisted in *peacetime* without special permission obtained from the Adjutant General's Office. This prohibition did not apply to soldiers who married and chose to re-enlist.[4]

The Regulations of the Army of the United States, 1901 continued the official discouragement of married enlisted men by stating that the enlistment or re-enlistment of married men for the line of the army was to be deterred and would be permitted only for some good reason in the public interest: "the efficiency of the service to be the first consideration." Captain James A. Moss wrote in his *Officers' Manual, 1907* that enlisted men who married without the consent of their company commanders would forfeit extra privileges which were sometimes granted to married soldiers, and their wives might be excluded from residence inside the garrison.[5]

Throughout the period of the Indian Wars, an enlisted man who wished to marry usually asked the permission of his company commander. If that officer assented, the soldier received certain considerations denied unmarried enlisted men. Whenever quarters were available he could live with his wife on post or else he was allowed to reside with her outside the garrison. The married enlisted man ate at home instead of having to attend the company mess. The soldier's wife frequently received authorization to work on the military reservation either as a household servant or as a company laundress.[6]

The soldier who married without approval usually kept his marriage a secret because such action smacked of insubordination. One commanding officer went so far as to recommend that in peacetime a soldier who married during his tour of duty be subjected to a severe penalty, one equivalent to that incurred for desertion.[7] A 7th Cavalryman, Jacob Horner, covertly married Catherine Stuart on April 18, 1880, at Fort Totten, Dakota Territory. They kept their marriage secret until his enlistment expired. Horner, then, wanted to re-enlist, but his wife persuaded him not to do so.[8]

The qualtiy of quarters assigned enlisted men varied from post to post and depended on the same factors as determined the quality of post construction in general. In March, 1879, the post surgeon stationed at Camp Supply reported that non-commissioned officers and married men's quarters were "insufficient for requirements," and that they "necessitated much overcrowding and in some cases the use of tents for quarters." The laundresses and married soldiers lived in tents at Fort Sill in 1870. As late as 1875, at Fort Dodge, the married soldiers and laundresses resided in dugouts or sod buildings along the river bank. Housing at Fort Lyon could be considered somewhat superior to that at Fort Dodge because there the married enlisted men and laundresses inhabited "old frame shanties and stone buildings."[9]

In 1874, married enlisted men at Camp McDowell occupied adobe huts covered and surrounded with brush. These dwellings, located some distance east of the enlisted men's quarters, "were miserable tumble-down hovels" which had been built when the post was first established. The post surgeon summed them up as "unfit to live in." Fort Yuma, California, offered the same type of adobe huts "which are unworthy of the name of buildings and utterly unfit for the purpose for which they are used."[10]

The post surgeon at Jefferson Barracks, Missouri, described the accommodations there provided for the laundresses and married soldiers as composed of one long building, formerly occupied by the soldiers, and two other smaller comfortable buildings. The long building had been so divided that each family had one large room, containing almost 380 square feet. That room had been partitioned into a sitting room and a bedroom. Cooking and washing areas were located in the basement. The post surgeon observed: "I have never elsewhere seen laundresses so well provided for."[11]

As the federal government continued its policy of economy and kept reducing the strength of the army and military appropriations, the army initiated measures that further discouraged enlisted men from marrying. Privates, making thirteen dollars a month, could not afford private housing. Circular No. 6 of 1883 clarified the governmental position on private quarters for married enlisted men. The Circular stated that the right of married soldiers to separate housing ended on June 18, 1883, and that any allowance to such quarters would be a "matter of indulgence only." In the future, no expenditure of funds would be made on these quarters "solely on account of their occupancy." The War Department further discouraged married soldiers from re-enlisting by putting into effect Circular No. 8, September, 1887. According to this circular, the Quartermaster's Department would no longer provide free transportation for soldiers' families.[12]

Lieutenant General William T. Sherman spoke for all married soldiers when he bluntly asked the House Committee on Military

55

Affairs: "Does Congress wish to prohibit marriage in the Army? If so, why not meet the question?"[13] No direct prohibition ever came from the government during the period of the Indian Wars, but Congress and the War Department added many impediments and frustrations to the lives of enlisted men who chose to marry.

Because of their general lack of education and their social position, very few enlisted men's wives left their memoirs. The reminiscences that have survived usually are sketchy in detail and generally exist in the form of interviews rather than as written memoirs. One of the enlisted men's spouses who recorded her reminiscences was Rachel Loback who was born in Carlisle, Pennsylvania, in 1858. After the Civil War she moved west with her sister, mother, and stepfather, Addison J. House, a first sergeant in I Company of the 2nd Cavalry in 1865. They traveled by train to Hastings, Nebraska, and then on to Fort McPherson by army ambulance. The family remained at Fort McPherson for six months during which they observed the many Indians who lived just outside the garrison. Young Rachel excited the admiration of the Indians who expressed great interest in her long braids.

Sergeant House was ordered to Fort Omaha where his family stayed a year before he was again transferred, this time to Fort Sanders, Wyoming Territory. Since no quarters awaited them, they lived in a government office building with two other families. In 1867, the Houses again moved to Medicine Bow, Wyoming Territory. At this time the army was engaged in protecting the construction of the Union Pacific being built just west of Medicine Bow. While at this station on the railroad, Rachel became a friend of Liza Lang, the daughter of one of the section bosses of the railroad. One day she and Liza went wading in the Medicine Bow River and were surprised by some Indian braves who appeared on the opposite bank. The Indians did not attempt to approach the young girls but waved their arms and yelled, "Wo ho, Wo ho!" The youngsters fled to the safety of the post.

In 1874, Rachel married Henry F. Brown of F Company, 4th Infantry, and went with him to the Red Cloud Agency. Since they could not obtain quarters, they lived in a log cabin. Mrs. Brown hired an Indian, known as Cheyenne Fannie, to help with the laundry. Fannie had the bad habit of appropriating things, but one day she went too far when she attempted to abduct the Browns' six-month-old son.[14]

Although enlisted men's wives could obtain several days' rations at a time, their day-to-day menu quite often remained the same. Mrs. Fred Klawitter, the wife of an enlisted man serving at Fort Abraham Lincoln in the 1870s, ate bacon, beans, hardtack, and beef three times a week. She often expressed the opinion that a fresh egg would be a welcomed change; but, instead, she learned new recipes using hardtack and survived the diet.[15]

Another enlisted man's wife served as General Custer's cook during the Washita Campaign of 1868. Custer described her as the "awfulest scold and most quarrelsomest woman" he had ever met. The woman who had lived as a camp follower for many years "was perfectly fearless." She would brook no opposition; and her husband, though dauntless in battle, approached her with great caution. Once Indians fired on the command while she was preparing a meal. As others took cover she remained with her pots and pans and muttered, "Git out, ye red divils, ye."[16]

Since the War Department kept no accurate account of the number of civilian dependents with the Army until 1891, no way exists of determining how many dependents were claimed by the enlisted men in any of the previous years. Another complication occurred when several men shared the affections of one woman. The post surgeon at Fort Stockton, Texas, gave evidence of such polyandrous arrangements when he reported that only four of the enlisted men regularly lived with women on a permanent basis. Most of the other soldiers cohabited with women they called their wives, and sometimes three or four men claimed the same woman. The doctor related that, considering the number cohabiting, there were few children since only twelve of the enlisted men's children resided on the post.[17]

Soldiers' wives cared for their own children, kept house in the flimsy government quarters, prepared family meals, and often supplemented their husbands' pay by working as cooks or maids for the officers' families. More often, the enlisted man's wife sought employment as a company laundress because in that position she could make a regular contribution to the family income.

The American army inherited the institution of the company laundress from the British, and a laundress was the only woman who received any legal recognition within the military hierarchy. The laundresses, or "Spikes," inhabited quarters most generally known as Sudsville or Suds Row. Their housing compared with the quarters provided the married enlisted men. In fact, the government assumed that laundresses would marry enlisted men since the *Regulations of 1863* predicated the number of married en-

Fort Laramie, General View, 1876. "Suds Row" or Laundresses' quarters, located in right lower foreground across the river from the main post. Courtesy Fort Laramie National Historic Site, Fort Laramie, Wyoming.

listed men on the need for company laundresses.[18]

An act of March 16, 1802, allowed women to accompany the troops in the capacity of laundresses in the ratio of four washerwomen to each one hundred men. Over the years the ratio was changed to one laundress for every nineteen and one-half men. The captain of each company had the right to appoint the washerwomen. As one officer remarked: "It is the captain's privilege to make or unmake them [laundresses], it is sort of a right of appointment that he has in common with the right of appointing his first sergeant."[19]

Laundresses received quarters, fuel, one daily ration, and the services of the post surgeon.[20] The enlisted men and officers paid for their laundry at rates set by the post Council of Administration. On February 27, 1866, the Fort Boise Council of Administration met with the sutler and fixed the prices of "soldiers' necessaries," and also set the rate the laundresses could charge each month. In this particular instance, the Council decided that each officer would pay five dollars per months, and every enlisted man, two dollars a month. This amount along with the sum that each soldier owed the sutler was deducted at the pay table.[21]

Prior to 1874, post laundresses at Fort Sill lived in a collection of huts, old tents, picket houses, and dugouts east of the sewer outlets. Similar living conditions characterized other posts. At Ringgold Barracks, Texas, during the years from 1870 to 1874, the laundresses lived in tents pitched on frame supports and located at the rear of the company barracks. These tents were constructed from boards, barrel staves, and gunny bags. Since these quarters occupied a conspicuous location, they detracted from an otherwise attractive garrison. The post surgeon reported that the tents were too poorly ventilated and lighted and too cramped for healthful or comfortable occupancy.[22]

Laundresses served at the captain's pleasure and were subject to military law, and at least one laundress was court-martialed. During the 1820s a laundress named Hannah stationed at Fort Atkinson was charged with using disrespectful language to the officer of the day, Captain Bennett Riley. The court found her guilty and sentenced her to be discharged from the regiment. In an act of clemency, however, the commanding officer remitted the sentence and allowed Hannah to remain on post.[23]

Another washerwoman who incurred the wrath of post officials wrote to Major L.H. Marshall at Fort Boise that she had been arrested, charged as a murderess, and confined in the guardhouse for assaulting her husband with a tin cup which he claimed was an axe. She had to appear before an officer who ordered her drummed off the post under the force of fixed bayonets. She and her three children then lived in a cold house and had little food. A sergeant later threatened her with death or a flogging because she placed two of her children in an ambulance during a march.[24]

The story of Linty the Laundress illustrates that the washerwomen held their positions through appointment. In 1864 at Camp Cottonwood Springs, a sergeant approached the officers of F Company, 7th Iowa Cavalry, with the idea that the company needed a laundry so that the men might wash their clothes. After they had built the washhouse, the wily enlisted man next suggested that the company could use a laundress to do the chore. Naturally, he had just the right person in mind. A young woman, employed at a nearby ranch, met the requirements for the job, and the company decided to hire "Linty," a corruption of the nickname, Lengthy. She moved into the laundry and began scrubbing the wash. A few weeks later, the sergeant asked Captain Nicholaus J. O'Brien to marry Linty and him. Even though O'Brien questioned his authority to perform the ceremony, he assented. After the wedding, some of the men gave the couple a shivaree. The company officers soon realized that the enlisted man had used them to gain his own ends; and, at the first opportunity, they reduced him to the ranks. Linty, however, faithfully "followed the troubles and dared the dangers of the service." Consequently, she gained the respect of the enlisted men who grew to despise her husband.[25]

Without doubt, the most notorious laundress of the Indian Wars era was the 7th Cavalry's Mrs. Nash. Elizabeth Custer wrote that "Old Nash" joined the 7th Cavalry in Kentucky and worked as a company laundress. Mrs. Nash also baked pies, retailored soldiers' uniforms, and managed to accumulate a little money. The laundress told Mrs. Custer that her husband, an enlisted man, had absconded with all her savings. Without obtaining a divorce, Mrs. Nash, nevertheless, married another soldier and accompanied the regiment to Dakota. The laundress's second husband turned out no better than the first because he, too, took her money and deserted. Mrs. Nash soon attracted a third consort, who happened to be Captain Tom Custer's striker. Old Nash had also become popular with the women of the regiment because of her great skills as a midwife.

By 1878, Mrs. Nash had established a fourth liaison with a

corporal at Fort Meade, Dakota Territory. While the soldier campaigned with his unit, Mrs. Nash became ill and died. Just before her death she begged the women in attendance to disregard the last rites and bury her immediately. The women found it unthinkable not to pay final respects to a person who for so many years had cared for the sick and dressed the dead. In preparing the the body for burial, her friends discovered the secret the laundress had jealously guarded for many years. In truth, Mrs. Nash was a man.[26]

Enlisted men's wives and company laundresses faced the same hardships that the officers' wives endured on the frontier. Because of their relatively low economic and social status, these women experienced additional difficulties. Even Elizabeth Custer recognized this fact when she wrote:

It was a hard life for her camping out with the other
laundresses, as they are limited for room and several are
obliged to share a tent together. In the daytime they
ride in an Army wagon, huddled in with children and
baggage.[27]

The laundresses and enlisted men's wives met needs other than just doing the troops' wash. They served as part-time cooks and maids in the officers' homes, and also washed the officers' family laundry. Most important, though, the laundresses functioned as midwives and nurses. Mrs. Nash rightfully enjoyed her reputation as a gentle nurse and accomplished midwife. In 1874, Emily FitzGerald, living in Sitka, depended on a company laundress to care for her newborn son. As General J.C. Kelton pointed out to the House Committee on Military Affairs in 1876, the laundresses "afforded the only assistance on post when death or childbirth occurred in the officers' families." General Kelton warned that if the laundresses were phased out, "it must follow . . . the wives and families of the officers must leave most of our garrisons, and it is very certain in their stead will come immorality, dishonor, and dishonesty."[28]

Because of the military caste system, a great social distance separated the lives of the officers' ladies and the company laundresses. In some instances, however, the question of true identity arose. Ami Frank Mulford related an anecdote about an officer's spouse and a washerwoman who approached each other from opposite sides of the parade. Dressed in their finest, the two passed "each other with eyes front and nose up as if each thought she owned the whole reservation, with the troops thrown in."

Enlisted men and their dependents at Fort Davis, circa 1888-1890. Commissary Sergeant Forsyth is seated at right, holding the infant. Courtesy Fort Davis National Historic Site, Fort Davis, Texas.

Married Enlisted Men's quarters at Fort Laramie in 1884. Courtesy Fort Laramie National Historic Site, Fort Laramie, Wyoming.

Each seemed to want to look back and inspect the other's costume. The officer's lady yielded to the temptation, glanced back, and ran into a wheelbarrow that reared up and landed in her lap. After untangling herself, she jumped up, gave the vehicle a vicious parting kick, and stalked off. By that time, the laundress had disappeared.[29]

Elizabeth Custer recounted an episode in which a laundress clearly recognized the social gulf that existed between the two groups. An old Irish laundress chose to continue her military existence even though she received a pension as a Civil War widow. The old woman had been employed as a cook by one officer, but she became ill and had to relinquish her position. Although her former job had been filled when she recovered, she learned that another officer needed a cook. The officer had risen from the ranks, and his wife had once worked as a laundress. The Irish woman refused employment because, as she explained, "I ken work for a leddy, but I can't go there; there was a time when Mrs. ——— and I had our toobs side by side."[30]

Wilbur S. Nye, S.E. Whitman, and James M. Merrill have variously described the company laundresses as a rough lot living together in barely habitable quarters, and existing in a general atmosphere of squalor amid hordes of shock-headed and raucous children of dubious parentage, scavenging chickens, and prowling dogs. These washerwomen often became embroiled in fights, and the officer of the day and guard frequently had to intervene in their quarrels.[31]

General George A. Forsyth, more generous in his characterization of the launderesses, described them as "good, honest, industrious wives, usually well on in years, minutely familiar with their rights, which they dared to maintain with acrimonious volubility." Martially inclined, they were kind at heart, though rough in manner, always prepared to help when needed. The typical laundress was also mother of several children; and quite often the soldier-husband had to care for their children while his wife did her part of the company wash.[32]

In 1876, the question of retaining company laundresses arose during the investigation conducted by the House Committee on Military Affairs. This inquiry elicited two conflicting points of view from the officers questioned. Several officers, who testified that laundresses should be retained, tried to influence the members of the Committee by depicting these women as worthwhile institutions on the military posts.[33]

General George Sykes reported that the presence of the laundresses on the posts had a good influence on the soldiers who liked to see and talk to them occasionally. As he observed: "It makes them [soldiers] more contented." General J.C. Kelton reinforced General Sykes's point of view by stating that the laundresses were necessary to garrison life for greater purposes than as washerwomen: "It had been discovered ages ago that no community of men can prosper where there are no wives and children." He considered the laundresses to be superior women, and their children were "just as neat and charming as may be found in any community." He also believed that the "influence of these women and their helpless families is of incalculable advantage to the men of the garrison, cut off for years from home influences."[34]

Major General E.O.C. Ord recognized the salutary effect of the laundresses whose presence "tended to make the men more cheerful, honest, and comfortable." He concluded that the enlisted men enjoyed visiting the laundresses' quarters and partaking of the home atmosphere. General Ord recommended that the number of laundresses be doubled in those companies composed of black soldiers because the Negroes, "who are domestic in their attachments, . . . miss the society of women." The officer remarked that if transportation were denied these women they would manage "to smuggle themselves along any way and find places for their pots, kettles, and washtubs." Ord found the laundresses to be honest married women, wives of the best soldiers. He also warned that the discharge of the washerwomen would cause the resignation of their husbands because of the insufficient amount the army paid the enlisted men.[35]

Many officers, however, expressed the contrary opinion and found the laundresses a problem. Colonel Philippe Régis de Trobriand described them as an incumbrance on the posts where their companies were stationed and a nuisance when the troops moved. The question of quarters for the washerwomen caused needless difficulties and annoyances. Colonel de Trobriand stated that the quarters provided for the laundresses most often proved insufficient for them and their children. As the colonel remarked: "All these little tribes have to be provided with shelter, cooking stoves, etc." When the troops changed posts, the "transportation of all of the laundresses' paraphernalia, children, dogs, beds, cribs, tables, tubs, buckets, boards, and Lord knows what not, amounts to a tremendous item of care and expense." De Trobriand summed up his feelings toward women on the military frontier by suggesting that hospital matrons should be the only women allowed on the posts.[36]

Colonel R.I. Dodge and Captain Henry G. Thomas expressed themselves more forcefully on the subject of the laundresses: "Get rid of them!" stated Dodge. "It is an absurd continuation of a custom which grew out of other wants of the men of the company than washing clothes." Thomas based his objections to the washerwomen on the grounds that their husbands were in many respects worthless as soldiers because if their children became ill they had to tend to them so that their wives could do the company wash. He also held that "it is wrong for one man to have a large ranch and the comforts of married life which are denied to the other soldiers." Dismissing the argument that the presence of the laundresses exerted a "refining influence on the soldiers" as ludicrous, Thomas remarked: "I think photographs of the laundresses in the service would satisfy the Committee on that point." Finally, he described his fellow officer who found that laundresses created a humanizing influence as "more susceptible than I was, even in my early days."[37]

Another officer characterized the old soldier-laundresses as terrors in camp, and in some instances his description proved valid. In 1871, at Camp McDermitt, Nevada, Mrs. Cavanough, a post laundress, threatened to kill a first lieutenant with a knife because he had disciplined her husband for being drunk. A Mexican washerwoman, serving at Fort Bascom in 1866, was offended by a remark made by a soldier. She warned him that if he made another such statement she would cut off his tongue. The soldier took her words lightly and continued to slander her reputation. One day, while the enlisted man and her husband were asleep, the laundress severed the tip of his tongue. Marian Russell, who reported the incident, did not relate what disciplinary action the post commander took against the laundress.[38]

The numerous officers who answered the military questionnaires in 1876 and 1878, or else testified before the Banning Committee, estimated that the federal government could save several hundred thousand dollars each year if the services of the laundresses were discontinued. Commanding officers offered post laundries as an alternative to the washerwomen who consumed rations, and required fuel, quarters, transportation, and medical services. Although S.E. Whitman wrote that the laundresses "went by the board" in November, 1877, the House Military Affairs

Committee still concerned itself with the fate of the laundresses in the inquiry of 1878.[39] General Orders No. 37 of 1878 decreed that in the future women would not be allowed to accompany the troops as laundresses. A woman who was the wife of a soldier and now permitted to accompany the troops in that capacity could continue to do so at the discretion of the regimental commander until the expiration of her husband's enlistment.[40]

Women, however, continued to serve as company laundresses after 1878. Special Orders No. 122 of Fort Totten in 1880 authorized a laundress (wife of a soldier) to be provided with government transportation to join her husband's company. Circular No. 17, contained in the Fort Meade *Post Order Book* of 1887, directed the company commanders to inspect the quarters and conduct of all soldiers' families and laundresses: "No unreported visitors allowed!"[41] As an institution recognized by the War Department, the laundresses passed out of existence; but soldiers' wives continued to supplement the family income by taking in company laundry.

The true character of the company laundresses cannot be derived from the Congressional reports or the conflicting observations of commanding officers. The personality of the laundresses as a group must be assumed to lie somewhere between the raucous, rioting "haybag" of S.E. Whitman and other popular historians, and the somewhat biased opinion of an enlisted man who remarked that the 7th Cavalry's laundresses "were ladies in every sense of the word, and were respected by the common herd more than the wives of the officers."[42] Company washerwomen traveled west with their soldier-husbands; and in addition to all the laundry they scrubbed, they served other useful purposes as well.

Female household servants formed the third group within the plebeian society on the military posts.[43] The officers' wives imported cooks and maids from back East or else employed members of the native population. Attractive household servants, even unattractive ones, proved difficult to keep on the frontier where females were a scarcity. Often female servants married enlisted men and sometimes gave up their positions.

Officers and their wives felt certain responsibilites for the care and welfare of their female servants. Elizabeth Custer wrote that her husband tutored two of their maids who otherwise would have been without further schooling. Ellen Biddle exhibited a maternal regard for her maid, Mary Broderick, and refused to

Enlisted men playing chess in quarters at Fort Stanton, New Mexico, circa 1886-1890. Left, Sgt. William Meriseo; right, Sergeant Harvey. Courtesy Collections in the Museum of New Mexico, Santa Fé, New Mexico.

Sergeant of 3rd Infantry and friend at Fort Stanton, New Mexico, circa 1886-1890. Courtesy Collections in the Museum of New Mexico, Santa Fé, New Mexico.

allow her to marry until her suitor proved he could take proper care of Mary. Andrew and Elizabeth Burt took a young Mormon girl into their home and attempted to train her as a nurse. Christina, however, required as much care as the Burts' own children and had to be returned to her family.[44]

Sometimes officers and their wives endeavored to discipline their recalcitrant servants, and such episodes often had humorous results. Frances Grummond Carrington described an incident that occurred at Fort Casper in 1867. Mrs. A.H. Wands decided to "flail Laura (her black maid) into subordination by using a trunk strap." Mrs. Wands asked Frances Grummond to stand by and provide moral support while she administered the whipping. The skirmish between mistress and maid ended when the lady delivered a misdirected blow which struck the door. Laura hastily retreated from the room. Frances Grummond thought that Mrs. Wands would have been justified if she had gagged the sassy servant although the *Regulations* set no punishments for women.[45]

Mary, a young Negro maid, made life difficult for Emily FitzGerald. A precocious fifteen-year-old, Mary quickly became interested in the soldiers stationed at Sitka. Household chores bored Mary; she refused to follow orders and purposely burned holes in her clothes so that she would have an excuse to demand new ones. Mary also bossed the FitzGeralds' children and provoked Emily at every opportunity. When she complained to her husband about Mary's impudence, the doctor replied: "Get up and box her ears or I will break every bone in her body." Even though the doctor chastized her on several occasions, Mary refused to alter her behavior.[46]

The army caste system prevented close relationships between the officers' wives and the other women on post; but some ladies crossed the social line and befriended enlisted men's wives when they needed help. Emily FitzGerald gave assistance to a company laundress at Fort Lapwai in June, 1877. Mrs. Hurlbut lived outside the garrison; and, since she expected a child soon, she was afraid to stay by herself at night. Mrs. Hurlbut's husband had been killed during the first engagement against the Nez Perce in 1877, and she was left destitute. Mrs. FitzGerald wrote that after the laundress's child was born all the people at the post would help raise the funds necessary to send her home.[47]

Because few women lived on the military reservation, the soldiers sought the company of the laundresses and household servants. No woman was too old or ugly to have fun at an enlisted men's party. Elizabeth Custer described a company ball held at Fort Abraham Lincoln that was opened by the company first sergeant. The officers and their ladies attended and formed a set at one end of the room and danced several numbers. Then they adjourned to the company kitchen for a meal the soldiers traditionally prepared. General Custer thoroughly enjoyed his usual dish of potato salad, well-seasoned with onions. Afterwards, the official party returned to watch the soldiers and their partners dance. Women most generally came from nearby Bismarck, or were the officers' household servants, and the company laundresses.

The laundresses turned out for the dances and deposited their sleeping babies on the first sergeant's bed. They dressed in low-necked and short-sleeved costumes that "exposed their round red arms and well-developed figures." Mrs. Nash, costumed in a "pink tarleton and false curls, . . . had constant partners."[48] Another enlisted man's wife, whom Mrs. Custer nicknamed "Old Trooble Agin," also made her appearance at all the company balls but could not dance with anyone other than her husband. Her jealous spouse, however, "whirled her around the hall in an endless German Waltz."[49]

Enlisted men's wives and the laundresses, just as the officers' ladies, engaged in rivalries and petty quarrels although the picturesque scenes described by Whitman and others seem exaggerated. Laundresses did feud and fuss and sometimes required the attention of the officer of the day to settle their disagreements. As Jake Tonamichel, who lived at Fort Laramie during the late 1870s and early 1880s, remarked: "Soldiers, kids, and women fought — fighting was second nature." Casey Barthelmess recalled an incident which occurred at Fort Keogh during the 1890s. Two soldiers' wives got into an argument because one of them had burned her trash too close to the other's wash hanging on the line. One of the women threatened the other with a baseball bat, so the officer of the day asked an off-duty private to walk post between their quarters. The private, armed with an out-dated rifle and a rusty bayonet, solemnly kept the peace. The women almost immediately forgot their quarrel and directed their anger toward the officer.[50]

In their quest for female companionship, some soldiers formed liaisons with Indian women, and those arrangements upset members of Congress who found such conduct disturbing and demoralizing. The Banning Committee in 1876 investigated the morality of the various Indian tribes who themselves held different views on what constituted individual morality. Major General E.O.C. Ord explained to the Committee that some Indian men held their women strictly aloof from contact with the soldiers while others such as the Paiutes and related tribes in Utah and Nevada sold their women to soldiers and miners.

General Ord added that the Pimas and Pueblos, however, severely punished any of their women who engaged in any intercourse with white men. Soldiers, nevertheless, regarded Cheyenne women "as more or less loose and diseased," whereas Sioux women were reportedly free from disease. Both the Sioux and Cheyenne "have had intercourse with the troops more or less." The Sioux and Cheyenne women came to the posts and stayed around; but the official military policy was to continue "to prohibit the Indians remaining around the posts and thus prevent intercourses between them and the troops as much as possible." The officer observed in conclusion: "There is as much difference in morality and good conduct among Indians in that respect as there is among the different nations of Europe."[51]

Since soldiers who consorted with Indian women often developed venereal diseases, post commanders had to devise precautionary measures. For example, during the years from 1870 to 1874, syphilis ranked fourth among the infectious diseases prevalent at Forts Buford, Randall, and Stevenson. The surgeon at Fort Stevenson indicted the Indian women at Fort Berthold as the source of infection and recommended that the soldiers be prevented from visiting Berthold except on military duty and that the Indian women, except the relatives of Indian scouts, not be allowed on the military reservation.[52]

In order to guard against the further spread of venereal disease, the commanding officer at Fort Custer, Montana Territory, in 1886, recommended the immediate creation of a large and well-defined military reservation and the segregation of the soldiers from the nearby Indian women. Colonel N.A.M. Dudley reported that a group of worthless and lewd women existed among the Indians around Fort Custer and that two-thirds of the incapacitated men at the post's hospital suffered from venereal diseases contracted from these women. Since venereal infections were so pervasive during the 1870s, General Tasker H. Bliss wryly observed that a common saying in the Regular Army was "that [post surgeons] had nothing to do but confine laundresses and treat clap."[53]

Throughout history, prostitutes have followed armies, and the Indian-Fighting Army proved no exception to this custom. Sergeant Reginald A. Bradley recalled that the first people he saw on reaching Fort Bowie, Arizona Territory, from Bowie Station were a "bunch of prostitutes camped outside the post." Prostitutes — true "camp followers" — lived in nearby towns, at "hog ranches" just outside the military reservations, or sometimes within the post complexes themselves. On at least one occasion, these women traveled with the troops.[54]

In 1881, President Rutherford B. Hayes inadvertently lowered the moral tone of the military frontier when he issued a presidential order forbidding the sale of whiskey at all military establishments.[55] No longer able to buy whiskey at the post traders' stores, soldiers patronized "hog ranches" that specialized in "watered whiskey and wayward women" and sprang up over night just outside the limits of the military reservations. Jake Tonamichel reminisced that a "hog ranch" existed on the edge of the Fort Laramie military reservation where three harlots lived. The prostitutes "looked pretty, all painted up and in pretty dresses," recalled Tonamichel. General George A. Forsyth, however, decried these establishments which were totally un-supervised and whose owners sold the soldiers cheap whiskey, took their money at faro, and procured the most wretched and lowest class of abandoned women for the soldiers' needs.[56]

Elizabeth Custer wrote that a number of "whiskey ranches" were located just across the Missouri River facing Fort Abraham Lincoln. The Missouri River flooded during the spring of 1875 and inundated such picturesquely named resorts as "My Lady's Bower," and "Dew Drop Inn." Using field glasses, the women at the fort discovered that some women were among the inhabitants of these "hog ranches" and watched as one of the bawds got into a boat and was swept away. The rapidly swirling water, full of ice floes, precluded any attempt by military personnel at saving the woman.[57]

Prostitutes living on the military reservation caused many problems for commanding officers. Sometimes these officials resorted to radical measures to rid the posts of the presence of "daughters of joy." In 1852, wantons inhabited the caves over-looking Fort Union, New Mexico Territory, and infected at least sixty soldiers with venereal diseases. Major James H. Carleton, the post commander, ordered the women driven off the reservation. Military officers arrested two of these prostitutes, Jesusitta and

Dolores, and confined them to the guardhouse. Captain George Sykes and Doctor John Bryne decided to obey territorial law and parade the whores before the assembled company and whip them publicly. Private Alexander Lavery, one of their victims, received orders to punish them. At first he refused, but he reconsidered and gave them lashes that he rated as "trifling, slightly laid on." The officers then ordered the women's hair cut off and had them drummed off post to the blare of martial music.[58]

Although Captain Sykes's drastic action gained him a court-martial, it did not end the problem of immoral women frequenting Fort Union. In 1866, another post commander, Major Elisha S. Marshall, ordered a black woman named Cielia off the reservation because of her lewd conduct, and Annie McGee soon followed Cielia. Annie, described as a "vagrant and notoriously drunken and bad character, had been prowling around the garrison and entering the officers' quarters." A Mexican woman, Coruz Benner, formerly a laundress and characterized as a woman of bad repute, accompanied Annie. In March, 1867, an inspection of Fort Union revealed that gamblers and loose women occupied the "Old Post" and enticed soldiers there to "carouse all night." Major Marshall ordered the "Old Post" or "Star Fort," the "den of rascals and crime," destroyed.[59]

Prostitutes also created a problem at Fort Grant, Arizona Territory. There, in the 1880s, the post surgeon reported that venereal disease had reached epidemic proportion among the black troops. The doctor fixed the source of contamination as two "whiskey ranches" located just outside the military reservation where the gamblers and bawds gathered on paydays. Brigadier General A.H. Terry observed in his report of a killing that two brothels, located in Sturgis City, Dakota Territory, catered to the tastes and pandered to the passions of black soldiers. The brothels stocked black prostitutes — "negresses and mulattoes."[60]

In an interview in 1961, Johnny O'Brien, son of a soldier dicharged at Fort Laramie during the 1880s, related that a Negress named Oxily ran a "coon dive" just outside the post limits of the fort. O'Brien also remembered that "hog ranches" existed on both sides of the Laramie River and were frequented by soldiers who got overnight passes and went "to drink with the fast women."[61]

The morality of the frontier soldiers did not differ significantly from that of soldiers of other eras. As the military historian, Don Rickey, concluded: "Soldiers have always been numbered among the prostitutes' best customers, and the frontier regulars were no exception." Captain William Paulding gave his explanation for the behavior of the troops stationed at his post. At Fort Clark, Texas, in 1874, the soldiers' "amusements were only baseball and hunting so that at night they visited the town of Brackettville which was full of rum holes, and gambling dens, and lewd women, mostly Mexicans."[62]

Frontier towns catered to the soldiers' tastes. One such town, Winona, was situated across the Missouri River from Fort Yates and in its heyday contained nine saloons and a race track. On payday the soldiers went to town "to taste the night life offered by its brothels and their amiable hostesses."[63]

Women of all classes and for very much the same reasons followed the frontier regulars westward. Regardless of their position in the social hierarchy, women existed as a minority in the West, and most soldiers eagerly sought their companionship. In fulfilling the need for female society, the soldiers formed liaisons with Indian women and other members of the native populations and causal relationships with prostitutes.

Enlisted men's wives, laundresses, and female household servants, though separated by a broad line of social distinctions from the officers' ladies, endured the same physical and natural hardships on the frontier but shared few of the ameliorations which added to the glitter of military existence. Children, however, were one interest they all held in common.

Children of Guy V. Henry, Sr. Standing are Saidie and Thomas Lloyd, children by Henry's first marriage. Seated are Fannie and Guy V. Henry, Jr. Photo taken about 1879. Guy and Fannie pretended they were Corporal Daughtery and Private McShane. Courtesy U.S. Army Military History Institute, Carlisle Barracks, Pennsylvania.

4

GROWING UP
ON THE PLAINS
"Hallelujah!"

The government of the United States provided an officer with rent-free quarters, fuel to warm that abode, and forage for two horses. The food, clothing, medical care, and expenses of educating a family posed additional burdens to the officer, much less the enlisted man. A family often proved a luxury few army personnel could afford. Many officers chose to leave their families behind in the East or else sent them back to the States when they required formal education for their future well-being.

Colonel Philippe Régis de Trobriand observed that officers without private fortunes, forced to remain in the service for their livelihood, found themselves in the most difficult positions regarding the education of their children — especially daughters. Virtually no education facilities existed on the frontier posts during the early post-war period, and the families faced the choice of rudimentary instruction provided by parents or hired governesses — when such ladies could be located. A third choice, that of sending the children back East, was the course usually taken by military parents. If the children returned to the States, their mothers invariably accompanied them, leaving the officers-husbands alone on the frontier, deprived of familial comforts and saddled with the costs of maintaining dual households.[2]

Children, as did their mothers, fell into the governmental classification of camp followers.[3] No army regulations recognized their special needs; but, regardless of their fathers' rank, army children led for the most part pastoral existences. Fiorello

H. La Guardia, who spent part of his childhood on the frontier, described the western army posts as "paradise for the little boy." Because of the routine of the army garrisons, family chores were few and opportunities for adventures and amusements, numerous. The officers' children had enlisted men as friends and companions. Often the family striker filled the role of a glorified playmate. Guy V. Henry, Jr., related that Gibson, a young black soldier, became the family cook and his own personal confidant. On many occasions, his mother acquiesced to Guy's importunities and allowed Gibson and him to spend the day fishing.[4]

Contrary to James M. Merrill's opinion that "army brats rarely suffered from the childhood ailments of the cities," army children contracted the same childhood diseases as their urban peers.[5] They endured such communicable diseases as scarlet fever, whooping cough, measles, influenza, meningitis, cholera, and malaria which was indigenous to certain areas of the West.

An outbreak of communicable disease on an army post meant that the post surgeon had to adopt strict quarantine measures. *Medical Histories of the Posts* are filled with records of epidemics and the means adopted by the post surgeons to sequester the afflicted persons. In October, 1877, scarlet fever broke out at Camp Supply, and the doctor immediately recommended that the families of the laundresses be isolated from one another and that all visits between them cease. He further suggested that all hops and social gatherings be suspended until the disease had run its course. That December, at the same post, the surgeon reported that an afflicted servant had transmitted scarlet fever to Colonel William Lyster's child and that he had treated the youngster with doses of potassium chlorate.[6]

Surgeons at the various western posts recognized the relationship between poor sanitation and outbreaks of contagious diseases. On August 23, 1875, the doctor at Fort Laramie made note of a "considerable epidemic of diarrhoea among the children" and warned the post commander about the unsanitary conditions at the post — especially the company sinks. Post garbage and manure from the company stables also polluted the Laramie River, making the water unsafe. At this time, a relatively new means of disease prevention was undertaken when children on the posts were inoculated against smallpox.[7]

Many youngsters succumbed to the usual childhood illnesses, but those who survived existed in robust health and seemed to thrive in the fresh air and openness of the West. No childhood disease, however, extracted more pain and suffering than did malaria. This illness wasted away young bodies and taxed the doctors' ingenuity. Mrs. Frances Boyd recalled that when her son became ill with malaria he was stricken with high fevers. Whenever the youngster's temperature rose above 102°F., the physician plunged the child into tubs of ice-cold water and kept him immersed until he turned blue. The doctor then wrapped him in blankets and warmed him with hot water bottles. The Boyds' daughter also developed malaria and temporarily lost her hair as a result of the fever. Malaria accomplished what Indians and frontier deprivations had not been able to do because Mrs. Boyd decided to return East with her children.[8]

Guy V. Henry, Jr., prematurely born at the Red Cloud Agency on Janaury 28, 1879, also suffered from cyclic attacks of malaria which he contracted at Fort Sill in 1881.[9] His mother quite aptly defined Fort Sill as a Garden of Eden possessed by a serpent — malaria. During his first seizure, the post doctor treated the two-year-old with a teaspoon of liquid quinine every half-hour. Young Henry remained susceptible to recurring malarial fevers until 1890.[10]

That a child left motherless presented special problems to a father attempting to keep that child with him is well illustrated by the history of May Lillian Snyder. Captain Simon Snyder, Company F, 5th U.S. Infantry, married his fiancée on October 5, 1869.[11] Three years later, on Janaury 24, 1872, a daughter whom they named May Lillian arrived. Within two years his wife had died, and Simon Snyder found himself entrusted with the care of young Lillie. He endeavored to keep Lillie with him, but this proved difficult because he had to be away on campaign for extended periods of time. His mother offered to come West to keep house for him, but he gently refused her by saying that she could not survive in that country. "Why you would have no floors or bricks to scrub."[12] Instead, he depended on housekeepers and neighbors to care for Lillie when he had to be away. In a touching excerpt Snyder described one of his reunions with his child:

. . . at once upon arrival at camp where I saw my dear
little child . . . Lillie has grown so much during the year
I have been away from her that I did not recognize her.
She was very shy of me at first, but during the day made
up to me and talked quite a good deal.[13]

Lillie remained foremost in her father's thoughts, and on the eve of an expected battle with the Indians at the Poplar River

Simon Snyder in uniform, circa 1870's. He served primarily with the 5th Infantry. Courtesy of his granddaughter, Miss Dorothy Ronayne, San Antonio, Texas.

May Lillian (Lillie) Snyder, born January 24, 1872. Her mother died a few months after her birth, but her father took care of her on the frontier. Courtesy of her daughter, Miss Dorothy Ronayne, San Antonio, Texas.

Simon Snyder in later years. He was promoted to Brigadier General in April, 1902. After the death of his wife in 1872 he never remarried. Courtesy Miss Dorothy Ronayne, San Antonio, Texas.

Lillie Snyder as a young lady, circa 1890's. She was educated at the convent Mont de Chantal in West Virginia. Courtesy of her daughter, Miss Dorothy Ronayne, San Antonio, Texas.

Agency, late in December, 1880, the captain wrote in his diary that he hoped to come out of the incident all right; but, if he should not be so fortunate, then "God bless and take care of my dear little Lillie-bird as also my dear old Mother and my beloved sister." In what he entitled "Memoranda," Snyder expressed his last wishes in the event he did not survive the expected Indian onslaught:

> Should anything befall me during the time I am with
> Major Igles' command, my directions are that all my
> world effects be disposed to the best interest of my
> Darling Child, May Lillian. Anything in the way of
> keepsakes that Mrs. Martin may think the child would
> prize in after life I wish to keep for her. I hope my
> family may not be disturbed at Keogh until the season
> is such that they can safely travel, when I desire my
> child taken to the house of my mother to whose care
> I commend her during her natural life, Mother to name
> a proper guardian for her. At the proper age, I want
> Lillie educated in a convent, and it is my desire that
> she become a consistent member of the Roman Catholic
> Church.[14]

Fortunately, the Indian uprising did not occur, and Snyder lived to see his daughter educated at the Convent Mount de Chantal in West Virginia.[15]

By nature, a boy's life was much less circumscribed than that of a girl. Guy V. Henry, Jr., however, related that his younger sister often joined him in soldier games in which they took the names of their two favorite troopers, Corporal Daughtery and Private McShane, whom he described as the "two worst men in the troops." The soldiers, nevertheless, were the best friends of the children. Young Henry regarded himself as a member of his father's company and wore a uniform outfitted with a corporal's chevrons. He went to the pay table and drew his pay along with the other soldiers because, as he definitively stated, "I was a soldier." From childhood, Henry considered himself a man because men had been his nurses and they had taught him masculine occupations. Since he desired to pursue a military career, his parents thought that he could participate in all the activities of soldiers that were not physically harmful.[16]

Boys growing up on the western forts quite naturally played games of Soldiers and Indians and formed their own military outfits. Fred Sladen described his troop which consisted of his friends from Vancouver Barracks. They subscribed to the following oath by signing their names and adding "I do":

Know all men by these presents that, I the undersigned, do solemly [sic] swear that I will obey the orders of any officer who may be appointed over me and to serve honestly and faithfully and to perform conscientiously the duties of any office which I may be appointed during the time of my enlistement, which is one month.

John Howard, son of General O.O. Howard, perhaps in emulation of his father's scrupulousness, signed his name but appended: "I do — with exception."[17]

Although army children enjoyed a variety of amusements and recreations, they, just as their mothers, took greatest pleasure in horseback riding. Margaret Carrington related that young Harry Kellogg, son of Captain and Mrs. Sanford C. Kellogg, entered into daily pony races with her two sons during the march overland from Fort Kearny to Absaraka. Ellen Biddle's two eldest sons, Jack and David, learned to ride when they were only four years old. Guy Henry, Jr., received an Indian pony which he named Prince. One pursuit in which Guy and Prince engaged did not meet with the approval of his half-sister Saidee and her beau. Saidee, who had joined her family at Fort McKinney, Wyoming Territory, in 1889, went for daily rides with Lieutenant James Benton. Guy surreptitiously followed them and informed the whole family about their itinerary over dinner.[18]

Boys quickly mastered firearms. Fiorello La Guardia wrote that the youngsters at Fort Huachuca, Arizona Territory, in the late 1880s, were taught to shoot "even though they were so small that the gun had to be held for them by an elder." James Van Horn, son of Captain James J. Van Horn, received a 22-caliber Flobert rifle as a Christmas present. Being a novice, he chose the prairie dog as his most likely quarry. With great stealth he approached a prairie dog town, aimed, and fired at a choice target. The rodent, unscathed, scurried for cover. Van Horn, thinking that he might drive the animal out of its burrow, rapped on the mound with the butt of his rifle. Unhappily, the stock splintered and left the youngster in the unfortunate predicament of having a useless weapon and no game to show.

Van Horn also had a disastrous experience with his slingshot. He and a friend decided to perfect their aim by using the windows of two abandoned barracks at Fort McKinney as targets. They left no windows unshattered. The destruction of government property

Youngsters enjoying the summer of 1888 at Fort Laramie. Figure third from left is Reynolds Burt on his Indian pony Buck. Courtesy Fort Laramie National Historic Site, Fort Laramie, Wyoming.

Guy V. Henry, Jr., on his horse Prince, his Indian pony at the Department of the Platte Rifle Range, Bellevue, Nebraska, 1887. Courtesy United States Army Military History Institute, Carlisle Barracks, Pennsylvania.

brought forth the wrath of the commanding officer, Van Horn's father, who sentenced him to four or five days in solitary confinement in his room. He saw only his mother or the maid who delivered his meals. Van Horn remarked of his confinement: "No other punishment was inflicted, it sufficed."[19]

Fred Sladen gained his early knowledge of firearms when he and the members of his company fired carbines under the direction of Major John A. Kress at Vancouver Barracks, in 1880. The youngsters wore military caps and had uniforms decorated with red stripes. Sladen's experience with weapons served him well when he was called upon to act as defender of his family in April, 1880. A robber had entered the Boyles' house next door and awakened the whole household. Mrs. Joseph Sladen, upset by the episode, contemplated having Moyland, an enlisted man, stay with them at night. Fred wrote to his father who was away on duty that he would take care of the family. Since he had his shotgun and carbine beside his bed, he would "make a neat little hole through the first robber that enters this house at night."[20]

Seasonal sports and recreations occupied the children of the frontier army. In the summer, picnics and camping out were attractive ways of spending leisure hours. Mrs. Frances Boyd, however, remarked that the variety of insects in Texas made an outdoor picnic impossible. James H. Van Horn remembered a camping trip his family took, and how an incident which occurred on that trip drastically changed the life of one cat. One day during the outing, Frank Grouard, an Indian scout, carried a deer he had killed back to camp and began butchering it. Van Horn, impressed by the scout's manual dexterity, later tested his own skills on a garrison feline. The task of skinning a cat, however, proved too onerous, and the youngster kept the deed secret although no one ever questioned the absence of the cat.[21]

Baseball had a faithful advocate in the person of Andrew S. Burt who encouraged the sport at every post he commanded. His son, Reynolds J. Burt, recalled that one year during their residence at Fort Laramie his father organized a "Youngsters versus Oldsters" game and that he had pitched for the Youngsters. All the families on post turned out to watch the game.[22] Croquet and tennis also had their advocates among the military families of the West, and during winter the frontier garrisons participated in winter sports. Reynolds Burt related that the inhabitants at Fort Bidwell, California, enjoyed sleigh riding and ice skating; and on the days that members of the garrison went out to cut ice for the summer supply, a festive mood engulfed the post's residents. Otherwise, card playing by members of the officers' families and the enlisted men occupied off-duty hours. As a rule, the families played euchre, and the men gambled.[23]

Although army children rode, played baseball, went sleighing, ice skated, picnicked, and swam, their parents tried to have special celebrations for certain occasions. Simon Snyder wrote that Lillie observed her eighth birthday by having a party for nineteen friends in the hop room where they danced for two hours. With the passage of time, extension of the railroads, and increased settlement of the West, parents could offer their children a greater variety of entertainment. Captain Snyder reported that in 1887 he took Lillie and five of her friends to town to see a play. When they returned home, they found that the housekeeper had ice cream and cake waiting for them.[24]

During the early post-war period, with conditions on the frontier so precarious, holidays such as Christmas taxed the ingenuity of parents. Somehow they managed to secure special presents for their children. Simon Snyder wrote in his diary for 1879:

> Christmas Day. Lillie woke this a.m. to find her dear little heart made glad by the gifts of Santa Claus. I do not think she expected much but she found a very pretty tree, a stocking full of candy and a handsome wax doll in another besides a number of presents for her little friends, all of which she delivered soon after breakfast.[25]

Emily FitzGerald's children at Fort Boise, Christmas, 1887, experienced a very happy holiday season. They had a tree trimmed with ornaments from the previous year; and their father, Doctor Jenkins A. FitzGerald, made each of them a playhouse. Bert also received a wagon, and Bess, a trunk. Their maternal grandmother sent Bess a doll whose shoes were removable and Bert a set of toy acrobats. The children were given animals, magnetic toys, and some books.[26]

Fred Sladen not so covertly hinted to his father that he wanted a watch for Christmas. "The only thing I expect is a ——— . . . wa---wat-- you no de rest and I don't think I will get that until you get back." Reynolds Burt recalled Christmas, 1884, at Fort Bidwell. The Burt family celebrated Christmas Eve by singing some carols; and several families decorated trees with strings of popcorn, cranberries and paper rings since ornaments

Professor Achilles La Guardia (bandmaster at Fort Whipple) with at least two of his children: daughter Gemma, first, left front row, and son Fiorella, holding his cornet. At Fort Huachuca, 1896. Courtesy Fort Huachuca Museum, Fort Huachuca, Arizona.

Mabel A. and Thomas H. Forsyth, twins of Commissary Sergeant Thomas Forsyth, born at Fort Davis 1887. Photograph taken circa 1890. Courtesy Fort Davis National Historic Site, Fort Davis, Texas.

Charlotte and Charles Schnyder, two of three children born to Julia and Ordnance Sergeant Leodegar Schnyder. Photo taken in the 1880's. Courtesy Fort Laramie National Historic Site, Fort Laramie, Wyoming.

Sgt. Richard Flynn, Company D, 4th Infantry, wife, and children at Fort Laramie, 1880's. Courtesy Fort Laramie National Historic Site, Fort Laramie, Wyoming.

Group in front of officers' quarters, 1889. Officer at right is Lt. G.W. McIver. Courtesy Fort Laramie National Historic Site, Fort Laramie, Wyoming.

Ruth Hammond, youngest daughter of Chaplain and Mrs. Brant C. Hammond, seated at the family organ in their quarters at Fort Sill, circa 1900. Courtesy U.S. Army Field Artillery and Fort Sill Museum, Fort Sill, Oklahoma.

Family of Colonel and Mrs. Henry C. Merriam at Fort Laramie, 1888. Courtesy Fort Laramie National Historic Site, Fort Laramie, Wyoming.

and gifts were scarce. Kate Gibson remembered a special Christmas treat she had for some unexpected Indian guests. After the officers and their ladies left her home where she had given a hop, several little Indian children came and peeped through the window. Mrs. Gibson invited them in, fed them cake and ice cream, and found toys for them under the tree. The children repaid her hospitality by performing an impromptu war dance.[27]

Just as their civilian peers, army children enjoyed the special celebrations that accompanied such holidays as Thanksgiving, and the Fourth of July. Captain Snyder wrote that the children observed Independence Day, 1878, by shooting a few firecrackers. James Van Horn recalled that he attended the Johnson County Fair during the 1890s and that he had enjoyed watching the "horse racing, branding, rough riding and fancy roping." Fred Sladen somewhat mischievously celebrated April Fool's Day, 1875, by putting sugar into his mother's salt dish. Mrs. Sladen used some of the "salt" to season some meat, and Fred related to his father that his mother had been "aughful [sic] mad."[28]

Left to their own devices, the children created their own amusements. Fred Sladen wrote his father that some of the girls and boys at Vancouver Barracks had produced a play in which he played a French dancing master, Monsieur Adonis. Expressing a sentiment typical of a thirteen-year-old, he remarked that the play was "all about love and just suited the girls." Fiorello La Guardia and his sister performed at many public benefits. La Guardia played the coronet and his sister, the violin. Sometimes youngsters joined forces with the soldiers on post and created an unexpected entertainment. In 1884, Reynolds Burt appeared as a "surprise package" in a minstrel show and sang a duet of "I'm in Love with Biddy Magee" with Sergeant Mooney of C Company at Fort Bidwell.[29]

A few officers' sons experienced a unique form of recreation and adventure when their fathers allowed them to accompany the command on an expedition. David Biddle, age six, participated in the Modoc Campaign of 1872-1873. Because of expected bad weather, young David wore an outfit of heavy corduroy reinforced with buckskin and appropriate for hard riding. David also prepared for the climate by wearing a suit of warm underwear and heavy shoes. The campaign lasted much longer than expected, and David had to be re-outfitted with a new buckskin suit made by one of the Indian scouts. When the youngster returned home, he had an exciting story to tell his friends because he had been fired upon by the Modocs while fishing at Tule Lake. Instead of dashing for

Officers' daughters on horseback near Deer Creek, summer of 1886, at Fort Laramie. Courtesy Fort Laramie National Historic Site, Fort Laramie, Wyoming.

Captain William Davis and daughter. Photo taken at a fort in Arizona Territory in early 1890's. Courtesy Fort Davis National Historic Site, Fort Davis, Texas.

Officers, enlisted men, and children in front of Commanding officer's quarters at Fort Davis, 1875. Courtesy Fort Davis National Historic Site, Fort Davis, Texas.

Young ladies dressed for a "ball" at Fort Laramie, summer of 1886. From left to right: Lillian Brechemin, Carrie Merriam, Fanny Comba and Helen Warden. All are daughters of officers at Fort Laramie. Courtesy Fort Laramie National Historic Site, Fort Laramie, Wyoming.

Miss Mary Burns, daughter of a soldier in the 9th Infantry, at Fort Laramie, circa 1887. She later married Chris Nylen of Company C, 9th Infantry. Courtesy Fort Laramie National Historic Site, Fort Laramie, Wyoming.

cover as did his companion, he calmly strung up his fish before retreating to safety.[30]

Another outing ended less fortunately for Andrew G. Burt, the elder son of Andrew and Elizabeth Burt. In July, 1875, Andrew, then eleven years old, begged to accompany Professor Walter Jenney's expedition to the Black Hills. One day during the trip, a violent thunderstorm boiled up, and young Burt sought shelter under a large tree where a soldier had carelessly left a rifle resting against the trunk. A bolt of lightning struck the tree, ran down the trunk, arced down the rifle barrel, and struck both Andrew and a nearby horse. Andrew received a severe shock when the electric charge passed through his body and out the side of one of his shoes. The youngster, lapsing into unconsciousness, required the intense ministrations of the doctor for over an hour before he regained his senses. Andrew suffered permanent paralysis of one eye as a result of this accident. Had he not sustained the injury, perhaps he, too, would have pursued an army career as did his brother.[31]

Army children faced dangers in addition to natural accidents and childhood diseases. Varieties of insect, arachnid, and reptile life alien to the East infested the West and endangered their health and well-being.[32] Reynolds Burt related that the presence of poisonous arachnids at Fort McDowell in 1884 made it necessary for the individual to shake out his shoes each morning. The youngster's fear of these dreaded creatures caused one of the most uncomfortable incidents in his life. One night Reynolds awoke horrified because in the shadowy light he thought he saw a tarantula clinging to the sheet just over his stomach. Paralyzed by fright and afraid to make any sudden movement or noise that might disturb the spider, he lay rigid, almost too frightened to breathe. When daylight finally came, he realized that the deadly arachnid was "just a fold in the sheet." Reynolds emitted a great sigh of relief and a heart-felt "Hallelujah!"[33]

Army children growing up on the frontier usually had a variety of playmates although Captain John Bourke wrote that Johnny Quina, son of a Mexican laundress at Camp Beale Springs, Arizona Territory, during the early 1870s, associated with the "young savages" because there were no other white children at the camp. Bourke related that Quina "used to run around with them, in a condition bordering on nudity." James F. Walker, who spent several of his boyhood years at Fort Berthold, also fraternized with the Indian boys who lived at the Agency. Walker soon learned to avoid them if they "outnumbered him more than two or three to one." The Indians harassed James and his friend George Allen, son of the Indian agent. On one occasion the young braves ambushed the pair as they walked along the river bottom. George was armed with his double-barreled shotgun, which may have deterred the Indians from attacking the boys.[34]

Youngsters associated with the army took the rank of their fathers, and they knew of the social gulf that existed between officers' children and the offsprings of the enlisted men. Jake Tonamichel, son of a Fort Laramie hospital steward, reminisced that the "children of the soldiers and officers fought and did not mix socially except when they attended school together." Fiorello H. La Guardia, a social maverick in his youth, refused to recognize such conventions. As he remarked: "It never bothered me much because I did not adhere to such rules. I would just as soon fight with an officer's kid as I would with anyone else."[35]

Likewise, officers' children accepted the responsiblity of defending the family honor. Elizabeth Custer related an episode in which one officer's son came in to the evening meal with the story that he had been kicked and beaten by another boy. His mother asked if he intended to allow the other boy get the better of him. The six-year-old postponed retribution until after the meal when he asked his mother if he should change his clothes. To her surprised query of what necessitated so radical departure from the norm, he replied, "Because these might get all bloody." Mrs. Custer also wrote that young George Yates, age two-and-a-half, threatened an older antagonist with the taunt: "Got a pistol in my boot."[36]

Although strikers and other household servants performed services for the officers' families, some of these youngsters had chores of their own. Guy Henry, Jr., who considered himself a member of his father's troop, attended most of the dismount formations and often acted as his father's orderly. In addition to protecting his family while his father was away, Fred Sladen cared for forty-three chickens. At the age of thirteen, Fred assumed another aspect of the role of head of the house. He reported to his father: "I am the man of the house now. I carve the meat, I carve the beefstake [sic], roast veal and yesterday we had ducks and I carved them." He added that his mother had been somewhat reluctant to let him undertake that responsibility, but since he had done such a good job, she seemed pleased.[37]

In addition to household chores, army children also devoted

An Army girl at Fort Huachuca, 1884. Kate Grace Chaffee, daughter of Captain and Mrs. Adna R. Chaffee. Warmly dressed against the spring chill, Kate was eight years old. Courtesy of her son, Col. Anda Chaffee Hamilton, USA (Retired).

Captain Robert G. Smither, of the 10th Cavalry, and his son Henry, taken late 1870's, site unknown. Young Henry later went to West Point and was assigned to the 8th Cavalry in 1897. Courtesy Fort Davis National Historic Site, Fort Davis, Texas.

several hours each day to attending school during the regular school term. As can be expected, the quality of educational facilities varied according to the time period in question and the relative remoteness of the frontier post. Reynolds Burt remembered that no school existed at Fort Bidwell in 1882 and that his mother held "sketchy classes" for him. She also cared for his spiritual development by conducting Sunday School classes for all the children of the garrison. Later, in 1884, a school was established in the recreation hall at Fort Bidwell, and approximately ten children attended the sessions. Reynolds recalled that "an Irish soldier named Delany, of stolid mien but with twinkling eyes," taught the lessons. Martha Summerhayes wrote that a soldier, also named Delany, attempted to teach the children at Fort Niobrara, Nebraska, in 1887. The children, however, spent "all their spare time in planning tricks to be played upon poor Delany."[38]

Post schools, authorized by the act of 1866 which reorganized the army, led precarious and unregimented existences until the revision of *Army Regulations* in 1881 set forth educational guidelines to be followed by all post commanders. The school facilities at Fort Laramie in 1868 may be considered typical of army schools in the late 1860s and early 1870s. According to the post surgeon, the chaplain at Fort Laramie conducted a school for the children of the post and held classes at night during the winter months for the soldiers who wished to attend.[39]

The *Regulations of the Army of the United States of 1881* established the structure of post schools. The *Regulations* specified that schools should "be established at all posts, garrisons, and permanent camps" so that enlisted men might be instructed in "common English branches of education and especially in history of the United States." The *Regulations* invested control of the schools and teachers in the post commanders who detailed qualified soldiers to teach in the schools. Soldiers acting as teachers received extra-duty pay amounting to thirty-five cents per day.[40]

The *Regulations, 1881* recognized the social hierarchy existent on the posts by making school attendance of officers' children optional with their parents. Enlisted men's children, however, had to attend, and all children were to be washed and cleanly dressed.[41] Children went to class from 9:30 a.m. to 12 m. and from 1:00 p.m. to 3:00 p.m., five days a week. Citizens from the surrounding area could send their children to the post school, but they were expected to make a token payment to the post fund. Officers and citizens furnished the books their children used.

When classes assembled, the teacher checked the roll and had the absences investigated. He asked the orderly at headquarters to go to the homes of the officers whose children were absent and to request that they be sent to school immediately. The orderly presented himself at the enlisted men's quarters and required that their absent children attend the classes. If an officer chose not to send his children to the post school, he was ordered to keep them from playing or making any disturbance on the parade ground while the school was in session. The *Regulations of 1881* further stated explicitly that no favoritism to the officers' children would be allowed and that the post commander's children should attend the school and set examples for the other students in "obedience to the teacher and in deportment generally."[42]

The teacher had no authority to administer corporal punishment, but he could discipline obstreperous scholars by turning them toward the wall or by forcing them to stand in the corner. Furthermore, a child could be punished by having to wear the dunce-cap. If such measures did not deter the student, the teacher called upon the post adjutant for succor. If the child were an officer's offspring, the adjutant addressed a note to the parents and asked that they take measures to correct the situation and guarantee future good behavior. An officer's child who continued to misbehave was subject to a week's suspension from classes; and upon recurrence of bad behavior, he was expelled from school. If the child of an enlisted man broke the rules, the adjutant sent for his parents and instructed them to prevent a second incident. The *Regulations,* however, established that enlisted men's children were not to be expelled but "corrected from time to time until good behavior resulted."[43]

The governmental regulations set forth the guidelines for school facilities; but, as in so many instances, the divergence between educational theory and practice loomed large indeed. Johnny O'Brien recalled that the officers' children at Fort Laramie attended classes separate from those conducted for the enlisted men's children. He further reminisced that a soldier taught the classes at Fort Laramie during the 1880s. O'Brien, who later attended school in Cheyenne, failed to take advantage of educational opportunities. He somewhat ruefully remarked: "In fact, I never got much learning, it was my own fault, because I could have went, but I just didn't do it." Instead of going to school, he would while away his days "— just like any of the rest of the

Grace (on left) and Blanche Hammond, daughters of Chaplain Hammond, Fort Sill, Indian Territory, circa 1900. Courtesy U.S. Army Field Artillery and Fort Sill Museum.

From left: Miss Blanche Hammond, William H. Quinette, later her husband, Miss Grace Hammond, and Gerald Hammond, seated around a game table in Chaplain Hammond's quarters at Fort Sill, circa 1900. Courtesy U.S. Army Field Artillery and Fort Sill Museum.

Commissary Sergeant Thomas Hall Forsyth and his family at Fort Davis, Texas 1888-1889. All are children of the Sergeant and his wife, Mary Elizabeth, except their niece Beulah Rolhouse, who is standing directly behind her uncle. Courtesy Fort Davis National Historic Site, Fort Davis, Texas.

children, putter around and put in my time." Jake Tonamichel also attended the classes held at Fort Laramie during the 1870s and was exposed to a soldier-teacher who during recess taught his students how to become detectives. Tonamichel summed up the merits of his teacher by stating that "he was just a soldier, but he was a good teacher." Tonamichel further related how an instructor canceled his contract: "If a teacher didn't want to teach, he got drunk and lost his job."[44]

Guy Henry, Jr., recalled the school year at Fort McKinney in 1889. Part of that year, the black chaplain taught the classes; but, more often, the principal teachers were two black soldiers — deserters who wore "heavy iron shackles around their ankles." The chains that bound their legs together were lifted off the floor by ropes tied to their belts behind.[45]

In his letters to his father, Fred Sladen told of his school experiences. He wrote that, because of an outbreak of diphtheria at Vancouver Barracks in February, 1880, he happened to be the only scholar present at school one day and had to recite twelve pages of history all by himself. Young Sladen reported some of the problems besetting his teacher. The instructor, who had been encountering disciplinary problems in his classes, remarked that "on Monday" he had conducted his best session in a long time because "he could do something when he didn't have anybody to jump up and contradict every word he said."[46]

Captain John Bourke recalled another instance in which a mischievous student made life miserable for the schoolmaster. The post chaplain at Whipple Barracks, Arizona Territory, during the late 1870s, the Reverend Alexander Gilmore, also taught school in nearby Prescott. Bourke described the institution as a miniature Bedlam; the worst imp in the whole group was Dick Dana, the "bright and bold" son of Major James Jackson Dana. Young Dana and the master did not get along because Dick believed that "Old Gilmore was down on him."

One day the chaplain accused Dick of "lamming one of his schoolmates over the head with a spitgob." Even though Dick denied the misdeed, he submitted to the punishment of standing behind the master's chair and wearing the fool's cap. When the other students saw young Dana meekly yielding to the punishment, they quietly resumed their lessons. With peace thus restored, the master settled back in his chair and soon was nodding perceptively. Gradually, his brown wig slipped awry.

Dick Dana had long awaited this moment. With a warhoop

reminiscent of an Apache brave, he snatched the master's toupée, rushed out the door, mounted his waiting pony, and dashed down the street shouting, "I've got ole Gilmore's scalp, and here it is!" Bourke, somewhat sadly, recounted that the other students later remarked: "We don't have no more fun now since Dick Dana was expelled."[47]

Because their fathers led a migratory existence, army children suffered from educational deficiencies. Guy V. Henry, Jr., recalled that during one trip home to Danville, New York, his family enrolled him in a local school. The school officials tested him and placed him in the first grade even though he was much older than the usual first grader. As he observed: "I knew little about reading, spelling and arithmetic, while I was well-versed in lightning, thunder, vapor and geography." Douglas MacArthur attended regular classes for the first time at Fort Leavenworth in 1886. He assessed his early school career by saying, "But the freedom and lure of the West was still in my blood and I was a poor student." Another frontier scholar, James H. Van Horn, graduated from high school when he was twenty years old.[48]

Army parents agonized over the future of their school-age children. Simon Snyder reluctantly sent Lillie to the Convent Mount de Chantal when she was fifteen.[49] Guy Henry, Jr., as a teenager, attended the Tivoli Military School in New York. Later, he studied for the West Point entrance examinations at the Bragdon Preparatory School in Highland Falls, New York. Their parents sent Edith and Reynolds Burt back to their grandparents in Cincinnati where they attended school. Ellen Biddle placed her two elder sons in a Connecticut boarding school, and she returned East later when the two younger children required schooling. Mrs. Frances Boyd followed suit and went back to the States because of her children's health and educational needs.[50]

In addition to presenting their parents with special problems relating to health, recreation, and education, army children frequently involved their elders in touchy social situations. William Leckie related in *The Buffalo Soldiers* the story of Lieutenant William Foulk's two sons who were known to the residents of Fort Sill as "holy terrors and seemed to have dedicated their young lives to the cause of promoting adult misery." Lieutenant William Paulding wrote about an incident with his captain which involved Paulding's children. They were playing on a stack of lumber, and the captain ordered them to come down. Instead, Gertrude Paulding made a face at the officer. Paulding tried to explain to his

Quarters of Chaplain J.A.M. LaTourrette at Fort Union, New Mexico, circa 1883-1884. Daughter Genevieve is seated to the left. Courtesy Fort Davis National Historic Site, Fort Davis, Texas.

Major Guy V. Henry, Sr., 9th Cavalry, at the Platte Rifle Range, Bellevue, Nebraska, 1888. Major Henry is mounted on George, and young lady in white is Major Henry's daughter, Saidee. Courtesy U.S. Army Military History Institute, Carlisle Barracks, Pennsylvania.

superior that, since she was a nervous child, Gertrude had probably just "screwed up her face." Paulding also reminded the captain that sensitive children were not accustomed to being addressed in the same tones the officer used with the enlisted men. He requested that the captain refrain from ordering his children about. The captain agreed, but retorted: "Very well, I shall hold you responsible for the actions of your whole family."[51]

The complexity of relationships between children on the frontier posts is revealed in the remark by Jake Tonamichel who recalled that at Fort Laramie enlisted men's children and the officers' children fought and did not mix socially except in the school situation. Then, they attended classes jointly only until the fighting started. Children, just as General Forsyth's laundresses, seemed martially inclined. The youngsters, however, reflected the attitudes and values of their elders and grew up to emulate their parents.

Army children accompanied their parents to the western frontier. They partook of the hardships and misfortunes of military existence, but they enjoyed advantages and opportunities their urban peers could only dream about. Even though they suffered from physical discomforts and the lack of adequate educational facilities, for the most part they celebrated their frontier life and freedom with an elan that permeates the pages of their contemporary letters, and their later memoirs and reminiscences.

Officers and civilians at Fort Davis, Texas, in August, 1889. Fort Davis forms a dramatic background. Courtesy Fort Davis National Historic Site, Fort Davis, Texas.

5

MEN AND WOMEN
"The reputation of a woman is like
the surface of a mirror — a breath
(of slander) can cloud it."

n the microcosm of the western military post, few
individuals enjoyed private lives, and because of the
"solitude of their mutual existence," the inhabitants
of the frontier forts had no secrets. The residents of
the garrisons knew the intimate details of one another's lives,
and as one of the army wives related, "Gossip, malicious and
otherwise throve."[2] In such circumstances, the most outstanding
asset to an officer's career was a wife who could adroitly maintain
her own personal honor while diplomatically advancing his career.
A commanding officer's wife had added responsibilities because
she was expected to set the standards of conduct on the post,
function as the official hostess, and receive all civilian and military
guests with equal courtesy.

Elizabeth Custer wrote that early in their marriage her
husband had impressed her with the necessity of receiving all
officers and their wives with equal civility. Because Custer believed
that dissensions among wives, false reports, and senseless gossip
could ruin the morale of a military garrison, Mrs. Custer knew
as little of the inside politics of any post where they served as
possible. The general also informed his wife that she should not
snub an officer's wife because of her social position or personal
reputation. All the other officers' wives belonged to their official
family and should be treated as such.[3]

In addition to remaining above reproach, some army wives
also defended their husbands' honor and reputations and sometimes sought to intercede with commanding officers in order to

103

gain their husbands' promotions or changes of posts. Even Mrs. George Crook is reputed to have pleaded her husband's case with President U.S. Grant. As reported in the *Arizona Sentinel,* Mrs. Crook attended a reception in Washington, D.C. in March, 1875, and while promenading with the President had asked him to transfer her husband from Arizona because of his health. Grant replied that the general's service in Arizona had made him too valuable to his country for him to be transferred to any other post and added, "He serves his country so much better when his wife is with him that you will have to return."

Mrs. Crook, not allowing herself to be discomfitted by the president's remark, countered that Grant was correct when he called her husband a great general. Crook, in her opinion, was a better commander than either Grant or Phil Sheridan because he had taken only two hours to reconstruct her, lately a Virginia Rebel; and after ten years' trial Grant and Sheridan were still failing with the rest of the South.[4]

Sometimes, a less politic commanding officer's wife could ruin her husband's standing with his fellow officers and men by attempting to dictate policy. Such a woman was said to "command her husband's post." Lieutenant William Paulding related an incident in which Mrs. Edward Hatch attempted to force Colonel Hatch to stop the gambling on post. Mrs. Hatch, whom Paulding described as a "terror," continued to badger her husband until he exclaimed, "My God, Hattie, I wish you would mind your own business and let me run the post." Paulding wrote in his journal also that he believed Mrs. Hatch was the model for the colonel's wife in Charles King's novel, *The Colonel's Daughter,* and that from what he knew of her, Mrs. Hatch must have made the colonel's life almost unbearable.[5]

In addition to pleading their husbands' cases before superior officers, some wives became involved in their husband's legal problems. According to Lieutenant John G. Bourke, Mrs. Lawrence Lucius O'Connor often intervened during her husband's periodic courts-martial. Though Bourke wrote that both O'Connors were great thorns in Captain Jerry Russell's side, he described Mrs. O'Connor as a bright, well-educated and literate woman. Her literary skills in addition to her shrewdness and tact saved her husband from many pitfalls, but O'Connor finally fell victim to the "operations of the Benzine Board in December, 1870."[6]

Occasionally, army women became involved in court-martial proceedings. Frances Roe related that she was to appear as a witness in a court-martial involving two officers on post, but, happily the court refused to call her out of consideration for her as a woman and an officer's wife.[7]

An officer's wife who became involved directly in her husband's defense at court-martial proceedings was Annie Blanche Sokalski, who attempted to help her husband prepare and conduct his defense. Both Captain and Mrs. Sokalski were considered by the residents of Camp Cottonwood, Nebraska, to be eccentric, partially because of Annie Sokalski's habitual manner of dress. Frances Grummond described her as a woman who wore a wolf-skin riding habit decorated with wolf tails which trailed to the ground. When General W.T. Sherman first saw her, he exclaimed, "What the devil of a creature is that? Wild woman, Pawnee, Sioux or what?"[8]

Captain Sokalski's problems aside from those created by his wife, arose out of the immediate post-Civil War situation. As a Regular Army officer, he resented the amateur, politically-appointed officers, and in particular, his immediate superiors, all of whom were volunteers. He refused to follow a specific order and pleaded illness as an excuse. He, however, would not furnish a surgeon's certificate as evidence of his illness: an officer's word should suffice. Though his superiors had him arrested for disobedience, they did not bring charges against him but placed a guard outside his door during his detention. Sokalski considered this action a gross violation of his rights and retaliated against his superiors.[9]

In February, 1866, General Herman Heath sent Lieutenant Seneca H. Norton to Camp Cottonwood, reportedly to investigate irregularities found in the quartermaster's monthly reports. Sokalski, however, suspected that Norton had been sent to gather evidence against him. The captain's suspicions were confirmed when he learned that Norton had questioned two former strikers about the Sokalskis' domestic life. Norton specifically wanted to know if the rumor that the captain beat his wife were true. Such behavior on Sokalski's part would provide grounds for charging him with conduct unbecoming an officer and gentleman.[10] When Annie Sokalski discovered that Norton had interviewed the two soldiers, she stormed into his quarters and called him, among other epithets, a "dammed dirty little peep." The captain followed his wife, intervened, and the quarrel abated for a few days.

The dispute again flared into the open when Lieutenant

A group from Fort Laramie enjoying a natural setting. Male figure on right is 1st Lieutenant Albert W. Johnson, 7th Infantry. Lady in white to his right is Mrs. John London. Courtesy Fort Laramie National Historic Site, Fort Laramie, Wyoming.

Officers and ladies at Fort Apache, Arizona, December 1890. Mrs. Charles Grierson is in center. Courtesy Fort Davis National Historic Site, Fort Davis, Texas.

Group of Cavalry officers and ladies in front of Quarters No. 126 at Fort Sill, circa 1890's. Courtesy U.S. Army Field Artillery and Fort Sill Museum, Fort Sill, Oklahoma.

Officers and families at Fort Fred Steele, circa 1885. Courtesy Fort Laramie National Historic Site, Fort Laramie, Wyoming.

Norton chanced to pass the shooting range while Mrs. Sokalski was target practicing. In tones loud enough for her to hear, Norton sarcastically remarked, "By God, when women go to shooting at targets, it's time for men to stop soldiering."[11] Norton's remarks caused the captain to demand satisfaction for the insult to his wife. Later, on April 17, 1866, when Captain Sokalski encountered Norton on the parade ground at Fort Kearny, he blocked the lieutenant's path and called him a "dammed dirty little pup." Other officers broke up the confrontation and charges were brought against Sokalski.[12]

On May 1, 1866, armed with Benét's *Treatise on Military Law* and supported by his wife, Captain George Sokalski appeared before the court. The Sokalskis planned to offer a defense in which Mrs. Sokalski would appear and refute the allegations that her husband had mistreated her. The Judge Advocate, however, found Mrs. Sokalski incompetent to testify in the case.[13]

Except for the third specification of Charge III, which stated that he had illegally taken money which belonged to the post sutler, J.W. Hugus, the court found Sokalski guilty on all charges. The captain was sentenced to be dismissed from service. However, the Sokalskis refused to give up. They managed to have the sentence set aside, but the reversal came too late for George Sokalski. He died a few weeks later at Fort Laramie.[14]

Annie Blanche Sokalski, free spirit that she was, returned East, accompanied by her thirteen dogs. She had expended her best efforts on behalf of her husband; and even though he reportedly had beaten and verbally abused her, she stood by him to the end.[15]

Two women were involved in the court-martial of Lieutenant Henry O. Flipper in a different context: one became the object of official harassment, and historians believe that the other was the indirect cause of the prosecution of the first black graduate of West Point. On June 15, 1877, Henry O. Flipper graduated and a month later accepted a commission as second lieutenant in Company A, 10th Cavalry which was then stationed at Fort Sill, Indian Territory. By the spring of 1880 he had compiled a distinguished battle record in the Victorio War and had been appointed acting assistant quartermaster, post quartermaster, and acting commissary of subsistence at Fort Davis.[16]

At Fort Davis, Lieutenant Flipper resumed his friendship with Miss Millie Dwyer, whom he had first met at Fort Sill. Miss Dwyer, the sister-in-law of his company commander, Captain

Nicholas Nolan, and Flipper continued to ride together at Fort Davis as they had done at Fort Sill. Later, Flipper maintained that all his problems stemmed from the jealousy of Lieutenant Charles Nordstrom who, prior to Flipper's arrival at Fort Davis, had enjoyed Miss Dwyer's undivided attention. Flipper also asserted that he was the victim of a conspiracy among Colonel William R. Shafter and Lieutenants Louis Wilhelmi and Nordstrom who used the fact that his commissary accounts were short as an excuse to have him dismissed from service.[17]

Lucy E. Smith, the other woman involved in the Flipper case, worked as his housekeeper. She was in his quarters on the day he was arrested, and the arresting officers also took her into custody. Colonel Shafter ordered her stripped and searched. On her person was found twenty-eight hundred dollars in checks; the presence of which she tried unsuccessfully to explain by stating she had placed the checks in her bosom for safe keeping and had forgotten to remove them.[18]

At the court-martial, Captain Merritt Barber, who acted as Flipper's defense counsel, and the Judge Advocate, Captain John W. Clous, both inadvertently called the housekeeper, Lucy Flipper, thus implying that she was either his mistress or his common-law wife. Lucy, however, told the court that she only cooked, washed, and ironed for the lieutenant. In answer to the question, "He messes with you?," she emphatically replied, "He don't mess with me. I do his work."[19]

Captain Barber questioned Colonel Shafter about his alleged attempt to bribe Miss Smith into telling the "truth." To the accusation that he had promised Lucy a house in the garrison, friends among the officers, and that he [Shafter] would visit her, the colonel forcefully replied, "I did not tell her any part of it or anything that could be tortured into it."[20] Naive and uninformed about her civil rights, Lucy could not defend herself. Lieutenant Flipper, in many respects, exhibited the same naiveté and trusted his peers to treat him as a brother officer and gentleman.

The court did not find Flipper guilty of embezzling commissary funds but did uphold the charge of conduct unbecoming an officer and gentleman. The black officer was sentenced to be dismissed from service. The Flipper case remains significant because, had he been white, the lieutenant would have been allowed to replace the missing funds and permitted to continue serving his country.[21]

Another black soldier had appeared before a general court-martial at Fort Concho, Texas, on May 21, 1874, and was accused of, among other specifications, threatening a laundress with a knife. On March 11, 1874, Private Andy Clayton supposedly went to the quarters of Mrs. Lydia Brown, a laundress of Company C, 10th Cavalry, and used threats to gain admission. He was charged with menacing her with a knife while saying, "I'll cut you if you don't undress and let me sleep with you."[22]

The court found Private Clayton innocent when two of the prosecution witnesses failed to appear and after the testimony of Private Jacob Bayer, Company H, 10th Cavalry. Private Bayer swore that he had become ill on the night in question and had to relieve himself several times. Bayer testified that Clayton had laughed about his many trips outside and that Clayton was present in his bunk during the time he supposedly attempted to assault Mrs. Brown.[23]

The abuse of alcoholic beverages created many problems with the discipline of both officers and enlisted men on the frontier, and as the text will indicate, led to several officers' being court-martialled for conduct unbecoming.

In the first case, Captain Thomas French, Company M, 7th Cavalry was court-martialled because of his ungentlemanly behavior with a laundress while on march. When French appeared in court on July 11, 1879, he was accused of going to an ambulance occupied by two laundresses and there reportedly drinking "whiskey or other intoxicating liquor with a Mrs. Egan on October 19, 1878."[24]

Captain French also was charged with getting into the ambulance with the two laundresses, driving to a ranch, and, in the presence of the two laundresses and an enlisted man, becoming so intoxicated that he had to be helped to his tent. This indiscretion supposedly occurred on October 24, 1878.

The Court found Captain French guilty of the latter of the charges and sentenced him to be dismissed from service of the United States.[25] However, in a letter to General Sherman recommending clemency, General A.H. Terry asserted, "But for his habits he would be a most valuable officer." Upon the recommendation of General Terry and a majority of the Court-Martial Board, President Rutherford B. Hayes suspended Captain French from rank on half-pay for one year beginning April 15, 1879.[26] According to the military's point of view, the captain's more serious offense was not his consorting with a laundress but

110

his becoming inebriated in the presence of an enlisted man.

In 1887, Major Frederick W. Benteen was court-martialled for much the same reasons as Captain Thomas French. Reportedly, Benteen had also become "excessively addicted to the use of alcoholic liquor."[27] Among other breaches of conduct, Benteen had insulted the wife of a fellow officer while he was intoxicated. According to the testimony of Captain J.A. Olmstead, Major Benteen had told Mrs. Bailey, "Your husband must have a hell of a time with you." When she asked what he meant, he replied that any woman with her eyes would make it lively for any man. Having delivered that cryptic statement, Benteen then stepped around the wall tent where the ladies were sitting and, not ten feet away from them, urinated on another tent. Olmstead testified, "We all heard it, I immediately got up and left, not knowing what might happen next."[28]

In Benteen's defense, his niece Miss Violet Norman told the court that her uncle had not meant any malice in his remark to Mrs. Bailey. She asserted that her uncle had only been teasing.[29] The court, however, found Benteen guilty of conduct unbecoming an officer and gentleman and sentenced him to be dismissed from service. Upon learning of the verdict in Benteen's case, fellow officers including Lieutenant General Philip H. Sheridan asked President Grover Cleveland to exercise the "full power of his mercy" when he reviewed the case. Cleveland agreed and suspended Major Benteen from rank and duty for a year at half-pay.[30]

A series of events which in retrospect seem like the script for an opera bouffe is revealed in the court-martial proceedings against Colonel N.A.M. Dudley. Colonel Dudley, somewhat misguidedly attempted to defend a young lady's reputation. In 1877, Miss Lizzie Simpson, daughter of Fort Union's post chaplain, accused Dr. W.R. Tipton of seducing her. Therefore, Colonel Dudley demanded that the doctor "make amends or at least restore the good name of the girl."[31]

This role of chivalric defender was quite out of character for the colonel since he had recently quarreled with her father and previously observed that Miss Lizzie "had been flirting with an enlisted man." Also, Dudley had taken no action to stop Lieutenant B.S. Humphrey who had openly spoken of "an improper conversation that Miss Simpson had with him regarding their past conduct together." According to the general opinion on post, Miss Lizzie was not above reproach.

The relationship between Miss Simpson and Dr. Tipton began when he invited her to a local ball on July 4, 1877, at the residence of Mr. S.B. Watrous in Tiptonville, New Mexico Territory. After the party, the young woman reportedly spent the remainder of the night at the home of the Reverend McHowland in La Junta. Accompanied by Dr. Tipton, Miss Lizzie returned home the next day. The couple continued seeing each other until July 23, 1877.[32]

During that period, the doctor wrote Miss Lizzie three letters which she believed offered evidence of his personal commitment to her. When her threat of "If you hear of my death, you may know it is on your account" did not force the doctor to marry her, she turned the letters over to Colonel Dudley. In an affidavit, the rejected young woman described the alleged seduction which occurred on July 5, 1877:

> You know I did not want to do what you wanted to do and refused to get out of the carriage, and told you I would not, and you pleaded with me. I told you I was afraid to do such a thing, and you told me it would not hurt me. You took your carriage blanket and laid it out on the ground, and took hold of me and lifted me out of the carriage. After you had done the act, you asked me for God's sake not to say anything to my parents about it and not to be troubled about it, that you would make it all right . . . you asked me if that was not the first time such a thing had been done, and I told you that I never knew such a thing before. . . .
> And Monday, July 23, I told you I was in trouble about it, and you said for God's sake say nothing about it, and you would fix it all right.[33]

Armed with the doctor's letters and Miss Simpson's affidavit, Colonel Dudley took it upon himself to restore Miss Lizzie's besmirched honor.[34] He called in several of his fellow officers stationed at Fort Union and told them, "A villain [Dr. Tipton] has seduced the daughter of a fellow officer. It is our duty to go there and try to prevail upon him to make reparations or restore the good name of the girl." All of the officers except a doctor at the post agreed, and they loaded up in an ambulance and drove to Tiptonville where the doctor then resided with an uncle. Between Fort Union and Tiptonville the determined officers stopped twice for refreshments to bolster their courage and make the task ahead more palatable.[35]

112

Upon arrival, Dudley had his fellow officers surround the house while he attempted to interrogate Mrs. W.B. Tipton who spoke no English. The young doctor could not be located in his uncle's home because he was at that moment hiding in a nearby cemetery. The doctor slipped out of the cemetery and went to his friend, John L. Bennington, who loaned him a rifle and shotgun and insisted upon accompanying him to his home in Boon Valley. When Tipton and Bennington arrived in Boon Valley, they found that the Dudley party had preceded them. Enoch Tipton, the doctor's father disarmed both parties, however, and bloodshed was avoided.[36]

In a direct confrontation with his accuser, Dr. Tipton denied seducing Miss Simpson. He flatly stated, "Whoever says I seduced that girl lies." Colonel Dudley then struck his breast pocket and pulled out Miss Lizzie's affidavit and the three letters Dr. Tipton had written her as he refuted the denial with, "I have the proof right here."

Dr. Tipton countered the colonel's evidence by remarking: "I deny seducing the girl. I have proof that the girl has been on it before, that she has made solicitations of the soldiers at the garrison, I have ample proof of it."[37]

With his son's denial of the colonel's charges, Enoch Tipton decided to return his son's weapons. Upon that development, Colonel Dudley told his companions, "I don't see that anything more can be done. Let us go home."[38]

The court-martial board found Colonel Dudley guilty of, among other charges, "conduct to the prejudice of good order and military discipline." The basis of this charge was Dudley's intrusion into the privacy of the two Tipton families who were wealthy and influential members of New Mexican society.[39] In this instance, Miss Simpson's "dishonor" was a purely personal matter to be settled by her family.

In one of the most widely known incidents in which a woman's reputation was involved, Major Marcus A. Reno faced court-martial late in 1876 because he attempted to use his authority as the commanding officer of a military post to ruin the reputation of a woman who supposedly had spurned his attentions. Mrs. James M. Bell, wife of Captain Bell, F Company, 7th Cavalry, resisted Reno's advances on two occasions, and Reno was accused of taking "improper and insulting liberties" with the wife of a brother officer. Reno also was charged with "taking both Mrs. Bell's hands in his own and attempting to draw her person close to his own." This "scandlous" behavior occurred on December 18, 1876. Then, on December 21, 1876, Major Reno in a second attempt at familiarity placed his arm around Mrs. Bell's waist.[40]

On Christmas Day, 1876, Mrs. Bell gave a party and, not wishing to endure the company of one who had exhibited such ungentlemanly tendencies, failed to invite Major Reno. Upon learning that he was the only officer uninvited, Reno furiously remarked to John Hazelhurst, post trader of Fort Abercrombie, "This means war! Mrs. Bell has thrown down the gauntlet, and I will take it up. Perhaps these people do not know the power of a Commanding Officer." He continued, "I will make it hot for her [Mrs. Bell]. I will drive her out of the regiment."[41]

During the period of the feud between Major Reno and Mrs. Bell, Captain Bell was away visiting his ailing father in Altoona, Pennsylvania. This left Mrs. Bell alone without a defender. The quarrel, however, soon involved the whole garrison because other officers became incensed over Reno's violation of their code of chivalry.[42]

The arrival of the Reverend Richard Wainwright further complicated the dispute because, through prior arrangement, the minister had planned to stay with the Bells. Wainwright did not change his plans even though he could be compromised by the situation since Captain Bell was absent.[43] As commanding officer, Reno believed it was his duty to prevent this impending scandal and advised Mr. Wainwright to leave Mrs. Bell's quarters and be his guest instead. Major Reno reinforced his argument by reminding the minister that he must carefully guard his good name because "Mrs. Bell's reputation is like a spoiled egg — You cannot hurt it. She is notorious in the regiment as a loose character."[44]

Major Reno further supported his case by relating that the names of Mrs. Bell and Wainwright had been mentioned by an officer of the garrison in the club room at Fort Abercrombie in the presence of several other officers. Reno stated that their names had been connected in an obscene and licentious expression. The officer, according to Reno, had remarked, "Mr. Wainwright would have his goose as well as another man, and he could have it with Mrs. Bell." Reno also informed the minister that Captain Frederick Benteen and Lieutenant George D. Wallace had requested that he expel Mrs. Bell from the regiment because of her reputation and past conduct.[45]

Wainwright refused to leave Mrs. Bell's quarters on the grounds that his departure would signify that he believed Reno's charges against Mrs. Bell. With Wainwright's refusal to comply with his wishes, Reno retaliated by stating that Mrs. Bell would not be allowed to play the organ at the scheduled religious services.[46] The commanding officer of Fort Abercrombie leveled all these charges against a woman's reputation at a time when her husband who normally would have acted in defense of her honor was absent.

Later, in their testimony at Reno's court-martial, both Benteen and Wallace swore that they never had requested Reno to expel Mrs. Bell from the regiment.[47] Officers present in the club room also denied hearing the obscene remark that Reno stated had been made about Mrs. Bell and the Reverend Wainwright.

C.K. Davis and Stanford Newell, defense counsels for Major Reno, introduced the question of Mrs. Bell's reputation. The Judge Advocate, Major Thomas F. Barr, objected on the grounds that her reputation was not pertinent to the proceedings of the court. However, defense counsel interjected that Mrs. Bell's character formed the foundation of the case: "Every allegation in these specifications either proceeds or it does not proceed upon the assumption that Mrs. Bell's character is not vulnerable or assailable."[48]

Once the subject of Mrs. Bell's character was introduced, the defense was allowed to enter testimony about her honor. Captain Benteen testified that Mrs. Bell had a bad reputation, and Lieutenant Wallace told the court that he had discussed Mrs. Bell with Lieutenant Benjamin Hodgson [killed on June 25, 1876 at the Little Big Horn], and that Hodgson had believed that Mrs. Bell "was not a true wife" because of several incidents which had occurred while the regiment had been stationed in Shreveport, Louisiana. Major Lewis Merrill also testified that Mrs. Bell's reputation had been damaged by her actions in Shreveport.[49]

In his summation, the Judge Advocate examined the instances in which Mrs. Bell had become the subject of gossip, and he characterized the danger of innuendo by explaining, "the lifting of an eyebrow by one person becomes a well-defined and elaborate charge when interpreted through three or four gossips — male or female." Major Barr also summed up the threat of such gossip to a woman's honor by asserting:

> The reputation of a woman is like the surface of a
> mirror a breath can cloud it. But from the mirror the
> vapor soon passes, and its brightness returns to flash
> back its reflection of nature. Let the vile breath of

slander fall upon a woman's reputation, however, and the cloud does not lift so thoroughly. The world is prone to accept the asserted for the established, and words wound cruelly when uttered against a woman's reputation, though she be as chaste as unsunned snow.[50]

The Judge Advocate concluded his remarks by observing that a man can combat scandal with "scornful indifference, but a woman has no defence save that which may be found in the arm of some avenging friend." When the wife of a brother officer became the object of slander, the responsibility of other officers was "to confute and resent that slander and not to aid in its circulation."[51]

Therefore, the court found Major Marcus A. Reno guilty and sentenced him to be dismissed from service of the United States. Because of Reno's past record of meritorious service, President Rutherford B. Hayes, however, commuted the sentence to suspension from rank and pay for two years beginning May 1, 1877.[52]

Major Reno had been back on duty for only six months when he was again court-martialled. In November, 1879, Reno appeared in court to answer the charge of conduct unbecoming an officer. Among other specifications, he was accused of peering through the parlor window of Colonel S.D. Sturgis' private quarters on the night of November 10, 1879. Miss Ella Sturgis, sitting in the parlor with her mother, was seriously frightened by his unexpected appearance at the window.[53]

At the court-martial, Colonel Sturgis, the commander of the 7th Cavalry, testified that his daughter "seemed in a great state of excitement and alarm and very pale" after the incident. He also remarked that Ella appeared in such a nervous state that both he and his wife feared that "she might be taken by something like Saint Vitus dance."[54]

When called upon to testify, Miss Sturgis told the court that the sudden appearance of Reno at the window frightened her so thoroughly that she could not move. She stated that the reason Reno scared her was that her father had only recently placed the major under arrest and that she feared some act of reprisal on his part.[55]

In his own defense, Reno testified that he had looked in the window strictly out of admiration for the young lady. He had not meant to frighten or harm her in any way. He swore that he "would rather suffer my right hand severed from my arm than harm one hair on her head." Captain Frederick Benteen, who

116

appeared as a defense witness, gave his own explanation for the major's behavior: he believed that Reno "was dead in love with the young lady."[56]

The court, unmoved by Reno's defense, found him guilty of conduct unbecoming an officer and gentleman and sentenced him to be dismissed from service. On April 1, 1880, Major Marcus A. Reno ceased to be an officer of the army.[57]

Since women were in the minority on the military frontier, officers sought the company of all women, whether they were the ladies, laundresses, or maids. Because of the military caste system of that period, they preferred the companionship of young women related to brother officers, or friends of officers' wives. Such young girls, unaccustomed to flattery and casual flirtations, might suddenly find themselves involved in relationships which would end in tragedy for all concerned. The court-martial of Captain Andrew Geddes in May, 1879, disclosed such a tragedy which effectively ruined the reputations of Geddes, Lieutenant L.H. Orleans, and his daughter Lillie.[58]

Captain Geddes faced the charge of conduct unbecoming an officer and the specification that he attempted "by persuasion, advice, threats and other means" to corrupt Miss Orleans to his own illicit purposes. The attempted seduction reportedly occurred at Fort Stockton, Texas, between February 11, and May 15, 1879. The officer also allegedly tried to abduct Miss Orleans from her home on March 12, 1879. Captain Geddes was additionally charged with "willfully and falsely accusing Lieutenant Orleans of the heinous crime of incestuous intercourse" with his daughter and of threatening to make this charge public if the lieutenant did not allow his daughter to accompany Geddes to San Antonio. Another specification stated that Geddes put his accusation of criminal incest into writing and made it public by sending a copy to Brigadier General E.O.C. Ord, Commander of the Department of Texas.[59]

Miss Lillie Orleans appeared as the star witness for the prosecution at the court-martial which convened in San Antonio on May 21, 1879. She testified that she and her father had arrived at Fort Stockton in the fall of 1878, and that she first met Captain Geddes at a hop in December, 1878. During a later hop in February, 1879, the officer squeezed her hand several times. A few days later he came to the Orleans' quarters while her father was away, and during the course of the visit, asked Lillie for a kiss. When she refused, he confided, "You do not know how much

I love you and have ever since I first met you." With that declaration, Geddes kissed her and immediately left the room.[60]

Captain Geddes, who occupied the adjoining quarters, started visiting her daily while her father attended either the morning or afternoon Stables. During these visits her admirer told her that he was unhappy, had not lived with his wife for many years, and that he had never loved his wife. He admitted that, although he had relationships previously with two other officers' wives, neither of them had awakened in him such a deep love as he now felt for Lillie. Moved at his protestations of love for her, she gave him her thimble and a gold cross.[61]

Miss Orleans also told the court about a trip on which she and her father accompanied Captain Geddes and Joseph Friedlander to Fort Davis, Texas, on February 21, 1879. During that journey Captain Geddes, who sat opposite her, covered both his and her laps with his cape. Geddes took her knees between his and kept pressing them throughout the journey. She also testified that he took the same liberties on the return trip. When asked why she allowed the officer such freedom with her person, Miss Orleans replied that she "thought if it gave him any pleasure he could go on without interruption."[62]

Miss Orleans continued her narrative by relating that on March 2, 1879, Captain Geddes visited in her quarters and attempted to take greater liberties with her. She swore that he propositioned her, and that he asked her to sit on his lap and kissed and hugged her. He then tried to force his hand down the neck of her low-cut dress and even got down on his hands and knees and begged her to allow him to kiss her breasts. Geddes also attempted to put his hand under her clothing; and, as Miss Orleans asserted, "He was so rude that it took all my strength to repel him."[63]

The ardent officer then asked her to allow him to wash and comb her hair, and he wanted permission to come to her quarters in the morning so that he might see her while she was still in bed. He also begged to be permitted to see her undress; and if she would not allow that, he suggested that she come to his room after dark. He promised, she testified, that "he would be so good and kind to me."[64]

To the question of why a young lady of her upbringing would allow a married man to take such liberties with her, Miss Orleans answered, "Believing Captain Geddes to be a gentleman, I inferred from all his actions that he would get a divorce and

118

make me his wife."[65]

Captain Geddes stated in his affidavit and testified in his own defense that on Sunday night, March 2, 1879, he saw Lieutenant L.H. Orleans having sexual intercourse with his daughter. While making his rounds as officer of the day, Geddes swore that he heard Miss Orleans beg her father to leave her alone. Since the Orleans lived next door, the captain attested that he looked in their bedroom and saw the lieutenant having intercourse with his daughter.[66]

According to Geddes' testimony, on the next day, March 3, Miss Orleans confessed her awful secret and told him that her father had been having intercourse with her since she was only thirteen. During that and subsequent conversations, she confided that her father had threatened her life if she ever refused him. According to Geddes, she also related that her mother knew of their relationship but was helpless to stop her husband. Miss Orleans felt degraded by her situation and begged Captain Geddes to "save her and take her away from this terrible life of shame." She stated that her father had completely humiliated and corrupted her and seemed incapable of leaving her alone. He did not even respect her when she had her "sickness." The desperate young woman confessed that in her despair she had often thought of "joining bad women on the street and going home with them" in an attempt to escape her father.[67]

Captain Geddes testified that he was moved by pity to help the young woman and had agreed to help her with the full knowledge and consent of her father whom he had confronted with the truth on March 12, 1879. The accused added that he had intended to take Miss Orleans either to her home in Austin or to his wife whom he would have informed of his true reason for championing the distressed maiden.[68] Geddes also refuted Lillie's testimony about the trip to Fort Davis in February. He told the court that during the trip he and Mr. Friedlander had observed Lieutenant Orleans fondling his daughter's breasts and heard her ask him to desist.[69]

A witness who could have offered evidence concerning the alleged incestuous relationship between the Orleans was not present at the trial. Private G.W. Sweat, Company B, 10th Cavalry, who had worked as the Orleans' striker, possessed knowledge about their domestic arrangements. According to Captain Geddes, Sweat could have told the court that Miss Lillie's bed "frequently showed that it had been occupied by two persons while the lieutenant's cot often looked undisturbed." On one occasion, Sweat reportedly entered the quarters after knocking and Miss Lillie's father "hastily ran to his own bed and his daughter lay on her back with her clothing in disorder."[70]

A witness who did testify, Corporal George A. Hartford, Company K, 8th Cavalry, recalled under oath that while at Fort Duncan, Texas, in May, 1877, Lieutenant Orleans "seemed rather more of a man that was newly married than a father towards his daughter." Corporal Hartford explained his reason for thinking an incestuous relationship existed between Lieutenant Orleans and his daughter was that he had "heard commonly reported that Lieutenant Orleans slept in the same room with his daughter and frequently in the same bed with her."[71]

Other testimony during the case established that the Orleans' quarters consisted of only two rooms and that they shared a bedroom with no screen or partition between the beds. The Judge Advocate General, in his report to the Secretary of War, made reference to this situation and emphasized that Lieutenant Orleans acted in a manner uncharacteristic of a man who had been accused by a brother officer of so repugnant a crime as incest. Instead of expressing indignation at the false charges, Lieutenant Orleans showed Geddes to the door, visited him in his quarters a few minutes later, borrowed money from him, and after the charge of incest had been leveled against him, requested that his accuser escort his daughter to her home. Orleans even went so far as to ask Geddes to pay his daughter's stage fare home.[72]

Since Miss Orleans' virginity posed a question crucial to the defense, three medical doctors examined her and testified that, so far as physical characteristics were concerned, she was a virgin; but they also concluded that no absolute or true criterion for virginity existed.[73] In his report to the Secretary of War, Judge Advocate General Dunn, however, advanced the hypothesis that Lieutenant Orleans had exercised great caution when he engaged in intercourse with his daughter and that he used a contraceptive sheath to prevent her becoming pregnant.[74]

After sixty-eight days of testimony which saw Miss Orleans physically incapable of returning to the witness stand, the court found Captain Andrew Geddes guilty of all charges except that of attempting to abduct Lillie Orleans. The court sentenced Geddes, therefore, to be cashiered from service of the United States and imprisoned for three years in a federal penitentiary. Generals Ord and W.T. Sherman concurred with the findings of the court.[75]

Judge Advocate General Dunn, as stated previously, raised specific questions about the extent of Geddes' guilt and demonstrated the incestuous tendencies in the relationship between the Orleanses. More importantly, the court had erred in procedures and had not give Captain Geddes a fair trial. President Hayes agreed with Dunn's findings and ordered the sentence set aside and Captain Geddes returned to active duty.[76]

Lieutenant Orleans, broken in health and partially paralyzed, retired in November, 1879.[77] The court records contain no mention of the fate of Lillie Orleans although it may be assumed that she returned to her mother in Austin, Texas.

One year later, however, Captain Geddes was once again court-martialled on the charge of conduct unbecoming an officer and gentleman. This time, however, the court found him guilty and dismissed him from service of the United States. Again, a woman was involved in the case. In a letter which Geddes wrote to General Abaslom Baird acknowledging the charges against him, Geddes deplored the fact that if he were tried a woman's reputation would be at stake. Cryptically, he stated that a woman who was "connected socially with some of the first people of New York and elsewhere" would be ruined by the "testimony of a monstrosity of the basest and lowest description, — viz, a white woman who had been living with a Negro for ten years. . . ."[78]

In relation to this statement, a significant question arises: if Geddes referred to his own wife, how had she managed to escape unsullied from his previous trial? The court-martial records of his second trial do not contain any mention of a woman in any manner which would compromise her honor, and no testimony is given by the woman described in his letter to General Baird.[79]

General George A. Custer had quite properly advised his wife about conduct becoming an officer's wife when he warned: "Dance, ride, walk, with whom you choose, but never allow any one officer to feel himself your special cavalier."[80] As the Geddes case aptly demonstrated, great dangers lay in such relationships.

One western historian wrote that infidelity on the part of officers' wives probably occurred "no more often than in the upper middle class at large." He also observed that while "extramarital affairs were not condoned, they were not unknown, including liaisons between officers' wives and enlisted men."[81] The reader is also reminded that such incidents as recounted in this chapter, though sensational in many aspects, form only a minor part of the total experience of army dependents on the frontier and were related for the purpose of demonstrating that improper personal relationships could damage not only officers' careers but individual reputations as well.

Rudyard Kipling, writing about soldiers who lived on a contemporary military frontier, made an observation about army wives which seems appropriate as a point of summation:

What did the Colonel's Lady think?
Nobody never knew,
Someone asked the Sergeant's Wife,
And she told them true!
When you get to a man in the case,
They're like as a row of pins—
For the Colonel's Lady an' Judy O'Grady
Are sisters under their skins.[82]

For the most part, women living on the western military frontier faithfully fulfilled their roles as wives, mothers and helpmates. Judge Advocate Barr spoke of the ideal when he expressed the chivalric responsibility of each officer to care for the dependents of his brother officers; but he also advocated an ideal cherished by his society in which honor demanded that each officer should protect a woman's reputation from the breath of scandal.

6

GLITTERING MISERY
"I fell to thinking:
Was the Army life, then,
only glittering misery?"

rmy wives followed their men westward during the period of the Indian Wars for much the same reasons women have ventured forth on all new frontiers: love, a sense of duty, the need to provide comfort and cheerful surroundings, and the desire to be where they felt most needed. Reassured by General William T. Sherman that the West was safe for their children and themselves, the women accompanied their husbands and aided them whenever possible.

Army women endured many hardships on the unsettled frontier. Their journey westward proved arduous enough, but the natural environment of the regions in which they were to live made their trip seem insignificant. Depending on the location of the frontier station, the women encountered floods, violent wind, hail, and thunder storms, blizzards, northers, and chinooks. Most army wives probably thought that more bugs, mosquitoes, arachnids, and reptiles inhabited the area surrounding their post than any other region of the West. Furthermore, the heat and natural bleakness of certain western sites depressed their spirits — especially when their thoughts turned to the more temperate climates and pleasant surroundings they had left east of the Mississippi.

The quality of housing available to army dependents varied according to the location of the post although quarters at most western garrisons during the immediate post-Civil War period were uniformly bad. Because of the scarcity of available quarters, new arrivals on post had the unpleasant chore of ranking out the previous occupants; because army custom demanded that an officer with senior rank should claim the housing occupied by any officer his junior. Although the women utilized whatever stores the quartermaster provided, they still taxed their igenuities to transform often drab, ramshackled quarters into pleasant and cheerful homes.

Officers' wives usually could afford to hire servants when such individuals were available. Often they had to settle for members of the native population or else send back East for suitable governesses and maids. The ladies soon learned, however, that the enlisted men eyed their servants as prime targets for matrimony; and after losing more than one, they decided to hire only homely or aged female servants. Many officers' wives discovered that the most available and reliable servants existed in the persons of the strikers — enlisted men who would work for as little as five or ten dollars a month.

Although army wives were vexed by the problems pertaining to the running of an orderly household, their major concern after worrying about their husbands and children was in regard to their own personal health. Most army wives shuddered at the thoughts of motherhood because they realized that the post surgeons were more accustomed to treating bullet wounds, snake bites, and hangovers than they were to comforting pregnant women and delivering babies. The women, furthermore, knew that in most cases they would receive the most competent care at the hands of other officers' wives, the enlisted men's wives, or the company laundresses. They accepted somewhat fatalistically the fact that if complications arose, their chances of survival were minimal; and even if their pregnancies were normal, they still could contract postpartum infections. Consequently, in those days prior to dependable methods of birth control, many army marriages were unhappy ones.

Although officers' wives considered themselves the most important women on post, according to the army, they had no legal existence. Of all the women associated with the army, company laundresses alone received official recognition. The laundresses, usually wives of senior non-commissioned officers, worked to supplement their husbands' meager incomes. Though they vocally defended their rights and feuded among themselves, the popular image of the washerwomen's raucous behavior must be labeled an exaggeration. The company laundresses fulfilled many necessary functions because they provided home atmospheres for the enlisted men, nursed the sick, dressed the dead, and

124

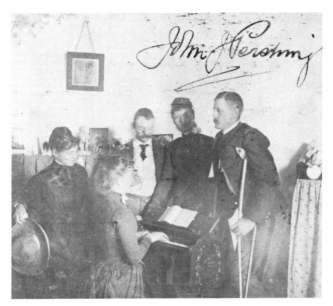

Group at organ enjoying one of the most popular frontier pasttimes — group singing. Figure at right is John J. Pershing. Photo taken at Fort Stanton, New Mexico Territory, circa 1890's. Courtesy Collections in the Museum of New Mexico.

Officers and their dependents enjoy an afternoon of croquet at Fort Bridger, Wyoming Territory, circa 1873. Courtesy U.S. Signal Corps, National Archives.

Officers and ladies of 10th Cavalry at Fort Assinoboine, Montana, circa 1895. Courtesy Fort Davis National Historic Site, Fort Davis, Texas.

Members of the Department of the Platte Rifle Team and lady guests at Bellevue, Nebraska, 1888. Young man to right of center is Guy V. Henry, Jr. His father is to his right. Courtesy U.S. Army Military History Institute, Carlisle Barracks, Pennsylvania.

Mrs. W.H. Quinette (née Blanche Hammond), wife of Post Trader at Fort Sill, circa 1900. Courtesy U.S. Army Field Artillery and Fort Sill Museum, Fort Sill, Oklahoma.

A lady visiting summer camp near Fort Lowell, Arizona, circa, 1887. Courtesy Presidio Army Museum.

offered their services to all members of the garrison in times of need. When no hospital matrons were available, the laundresses also assisted the post surgeons. In the investigations of 1876 and 1878, Congress questioned the advisability of retaining the laundresses. Although many officers recommended that they be kept, Congress, nevertheless, decided that they were expendable; and, after 1878, company laundresses retired from service when their husbands' terms of enlistment expired.

True "camp followers," or prostitutes, have accompanied armies since time immemorial, and the Indian-Fighting Army proved no exception to this usage. Prostitutes lived within the garrisons, at "hog ranches" just outside the military reservations, or in towns nearby. Whenever possible, soldiers also formed liaisons with the women of the various Indian tribes.

Regardless of their social standing, women on the western posts participated in the forms of recreation available. Of course, the officers' wives had greater opportunities to take advantage of the facilities at hand. They often invented reasons for getting together, such as the sewing bees, where they could finish the weekly mending and trade items of gossip simultaneously. Army wives enjoyed riding hunting, fishing, and the socials which usually took place on a weekly basis — especially in the autumn and winter months after the men had returned from the long campaigns of the summer. General George and Mrs. Elizabeth Custer often entertained nightly when a group of officers and their wives gathered in the Custers' parlor and sang favorite songs to the accompaniment of piano or guitars. Maids and laundresses were sought out as partners by the men at the company hops. No woman present on post was old or ugly enough to be classified as a wall-flower. Although army chaplains served only at garrisons designated as Chaplains' Posts, army wives attached great importance to Sunday Services and found consolation in their religious practices.

One interest common to all the women on the military frontier was their children. Unlike their mothers, youngsters led a pastoral existence on the military posts. They had few chores and could devote themselves to the usual pursuits of childhood. Boys learned to ride and shoot at an early age, almost as soon as they could walk. They often played games of Soldiers and Indians and had exciting adventures when they occasionally were allowed to accompany the command on scouting expeditions. Commanding Officers' sons frequently helped their fathers by acting as orderlies. Youngsters who wished to follow in their fathers' footsteps were encouraged by their parents to learn all about soldiering. Consequently, those parents permitted their sons to associate with the enlisted men.

Army parents recognized their children's need for formal education and sent them back East to relatives or boarding schools. After the *Army Regulations of 1881* established the post schools under the superivision of the commanding officers, those parents who wanted their children at home had an alternative for their offsprings. These children enjoyed a variety of playmates from young enlisted men to members of the native Indian and Mexican populations. They participated in the popular sports of the day and looked forward to the traditional holidays. Parents often taxed their ingenuity to provide recreational and holiday entertainments for their children.

The dependents of the Indian-Fighting Army followed the soldiers westward and tried to provide the stable homelife so important to the well-being of the soldiers. All the dependents faced the harshness of life on the unsettled frontier with its physical hardships and psychological strains. Because of their social status and financial standing, the officers' dependents could ameliorate their frontier existence. The enlisted men's dependents fared less well, but they also shared in the panoply and excitement of the dress parades and other formal military occasions. Nevertheless, during the period of the Indian Wars, 1865 to 1898, army dependents in the trans-Mississippi West shared an existence best characterized by the phrase, "Glittering Misery."

Ladies posing on steps of Lieutenant Ames' quarters, Benicia Barracks, circa 1880's. Courtesy Presidio Army Museum.

NOTES

Chapter 1
THE DISMAL YEARS

1. Robert G. Athearn, *William Tecumseh Sherman and the Settlement of the West* (Norman: University of Oklahoma Press, 1956), p. 43.

2. Piers Compton, *Colonel's Lady and Camp-Follower: The Story of Women in the Crimean War* (New York: St. Martin's Press, 1970), pp. 19-45. Mr. Compton vividly describes the lives of the women who followed the British Army during the Crimean War, the last time women were officially permitted to travel with that Army.

3. Frances C. Carrington, *My Army Life and the Fort Phil Kearney Massacre* (Freeport, New York: Books for Libraries Press, 1971), pp. 61-62. A debate exists among historians about the correct spelling of Fort Phil Kearney. The author has decided to spell the word as the women who lived there spelled it – that is, with the second *e*.

4. R. Ernest and Trevor N. Dupuy, *The Encyclopedia of Military History: From 3500 B.C. to the Present* (New York: Harper and Row, 1970), p. 905.

5. Athearn, *Sherman and the Settlement of the West*, p. 43.

6. Fiorello Henry La Guardia, *The Making of an Insurgent, An Autobiography: 1882-1919* (Philadelphia: J.B. Lippincott Company, 1948), p. 19.

7. Martha Summerhayes, *Vanished Arizona: Recollections of the Army Life of a New England Woman* (Glorieta, New Mexico: The Rio Grande Press, Inc., 1970), p. 19. Mrs. Summerhayes borrowed the German term, *glaenzendes Elend,* to describe her army life.

Chapter 2
THE OFFICER'S LADIES

1. Summerhayes, *Vanished Arizona*, p. 204.

2. Rodney Glisan, *Journal of Army Life* (San Francisco: A.L. Bancroft and Company, 1874), p. 101. Dr. Rodney Glisan received a commission as an assistant surgeon in the United States Army in 1849. He served on the frontier for several years before he retired from service in 1861. Dr. Glisan believed that the frontier was no fit place for women and remarked that unless he fell in love unexpectedly he would endeavor to trudge his lonely way as before "with no angelic hand to press my feverished brow when ill, or soothe my anguished soul when oppressed with harassing care. . . ." The doctor thought that the constant parting between "husband, wife and children is far worse than having none from whom to separate."

3. Summerhayes, *Vanished Arizona*, p. 20.

4. Elizabeth J. Burt, "Forty Years in the U.S. Regular Army, 1862-1902," Manuscripts Division, Library of Congress, Washington, D.C., p. 39.

5. Elizabeth B. Custer, *Boots and Saddles or Life in Dakota with General Custer* (New York: Harper and Row, 1885), p. 119-120.

6. Frances M.A. Roe, *Army Letters from an Officer's Wife, 1871-1888* (New York: D. Appleton and Company, 1909), p. 2. In her letters, Mrs Roe quite often changed the names of the individuals about whom she wrote. Whenever possible, the author has traced the true identities of these individuals and enclosed them inside brackets beside the pseudonyms. Grace Paulding referred to the army ambulance as "about the most uncomfortable vehicle imaginable." Grace Paulding, "My Army Life," The William and Grace Paulding Papers, U.S. Army Military History Institute, U.S. Army War College, Carlisle Barracks, Pennsylvania, p. 3.

7. Katherine G. Fougera, *With Custer's Cavalry: From the Memoirs of the Late Katherine Gibson* (Caldwell, Idaho: The Caxton Printers, 1940), pp. 15-22.

8. Although he had been breveted a major general during the Civil War, George A. Custer, at the time of his death, held the rank of lieutenant colonel in the 7th Cavalry. Mrs. Custer devoted the remainder of her life to perpetuating his heroic image.

9. Emily McCorkle FitzGerald, *An Army Doctor's Wife on the Frontier: Letters from Alaska and the Far West, 1874-1878.* Edited by Abe Laufe (Pittsburgh: University of Pennsylvania Press, 1962), p. 20.

10. Excerpt from a letter written by General George A. Custer to his father-in-law, Judge Daniel S. Bacon. Marguerite Merington, ed., *The Custer Story: The Life and Intimate Letters of General George A. Custer and His Wife Elizabeth* (New York: The Devin-Adair Company, 1950), pp. 167-168.

11. Roe, *Army Letters*, pp. 161-162.

12. Frances C. Carrington, *My Army Life*, pp. 143-189; Margaret I. Carrington, *Ab-Sa-Ra-Ka, Land of Massacre: Being the Experience of an Officer's Wife on the Plains* (Philadelphia: J. B. Lippincott and Company, 1879), pp. 200-236; Dee Brown, *The Gentle Tamers: Women of the Old Wild West* (New York: G.P. Putnam's Sons, 1958), pp. 49-58. The purpose of the memoirs written by both Carrington ladies was to defend the actions taken by Colonel Carrington in reference to the Fetterman "Massacre." Fort Reno was the first safe stop on the way back.

13. Second Lieutenant Charles O. Rhodes, "Diary Notes of the Brulé Sioux Campaign, South Dakota, 1890-1891." Archives of the Order of Indian Wars of the United States Collection, U.S. Army Military History

Institute, U.S. Army War College, Carlisle Barracks, Pennsylvania, Diary entries for January 29-30, 1891. Mrs. Paddock's brother, John J. Pershing, at that time served as a second lieutenant with the 6th Cavalry.

14. Elizabeth Burt, "Forty Years," pp. 132-133; Mrs. Orsemus B. Boyd, *Cavalry Life in Tent and Field* (New York: J. Selwin Tait and Sons, 1894), pp. 127-128; Summerhayes, *Vanished Arizona*, pp. 114-138.

15. Account of S.S. Peters who survived the Sioux attack at Crazy Woman's Fork, written in Omaha, Nebraska, July 6, 1908. Frances Carrington, *My Army Life*, pp. 73-81; Merrill J. Mattes, *Indians, Infants and Infantry: Andrew and Elizabeth Burt on the Frontier* (Denver: The Old West Publishing Company, 1960), pp. 115-117.

16. Burt, "Forty Years," pp. 140-141; Mattes, *Indians, Infants and Infantry*, pp. 117-118.

17. Summerhayes, *Vanished Arizona*, pp. 122-124.

18. Frances Carrington, *My Army Life*, pp. 153-154.

19. Custer, *Boots and Saddles*, p. 63.

20. Ray H. Mattison, ed., "An Army Wife on the Upper Missouri: The Diary of Sarah E. Canfield, 1866-1868," *North Dakota History*, XX (October, 1953), 217.

21. Fougera, *With Custer's Cavalry*, p. 173-178.

22. Burt, "Forty Years," pp. 101-107; Mattes, *Indians, Infants and Infantry*, p. 67-74.

23. Custer, *Boots and Saddles*, pp. 68-69; Ibid., *Tenting on the Plains or Gen'l Custer in Kansas and Texas* (New York: Charles L. Webster and Company, 1893), p. 109. General Custer, notorious as a prankster and tease, accused Eliza of going to any lengths to get a drink of whiskey; Summerhayes, *Vanished Arizona*, p. 63.

24. Boyd, *Cavalry Life*, p. 276-279.

25. Roe, *Army Letters*, pp. 66-69. For the privileges of rank, see Wilfred C. Burton, "The Novels of Charles King, 1844-1933," (unpublished Ph.D. dissertation, New York University, 1962), p. 95.

26. Burt, "Forty Years," p. 137; Boyd, *Cavalry Life*, p. 55.

27. Surgeon General's Office, *Circular Number 4, A Report of Barracks and Hospitals with Descriptions of Military Posts, 1870* (Washington: Government Printing Office, 1870), p. 469; Roe, *Army Letters*, pp. 6-8.

28. *Medical History of Camp Supply, 1869*, Vol. 166, Record Group 94, National Archives, pp. 6-7; Roe, *Army Letters*, p. 58; Robert C. Carriker, *Fort Supply Indian Territory: Frontier Outpost on the Plains* (Norman: University of Oklahoma Press, 1970), p. 137.

29. Custer, *Following the Guidon*, p. 227.

30. Burt, "Forty Years," pp. 90-91.

31. Roe, *Army Letters*, p. 58; Elizabeth B. Custer, *Following the Guidon* (Norman: University of Oklahoma Press, 1966), pp. 227-229.

32. Don Rickey, Jr., *Forty Miles a Day on Beans and Hay: The Enlisted Soldiers Fighting the Indian Wars* (Norman: University of Oklahoma Press, 1963), pp. 111-112.

33. Summerhayes, *Vanished Arizona*, pp. 214-215, 162, 170. William Gurnett assessed *Vanished Arizona* by stating: "She could have written a thrilling story, but there was Jack and the baby." See "Letters," *Winners of the West*, Vol. II (August, 1924), p. 8.

34. Custer, *Boots and Saddles,* p. 185; Boyd, *Cavalry Life,* pp. 54-55; Roe, *Army Letters,* p. 69.

35. Custer, *Following the Guidon,* pp. 227-228; Guy V. Henry, Jr., "A Brief Life of Guy V. Henry, Jr." U.S. Army Military History Institute, U.S. Army War College, Carlisle Barracks, Pennsylvania, p. 6; Roe, *Army Letters,* p. 55. Mrs. Roe did not care for black soldiers, about whom she wrote: "I can readily believe that some of them can be alert, and possibly good soldiers, and that they can be good thieves too. . . ." Ibid., pp. 77-78.

36. Adjutant General's Office, General Orders No. 92, *Index of General Orders, 1870* (Washington: Government Printing Office, 1871), p. 6. At the present time, the army is involved in a controversy concerning the employment of enlisted men by general officers. These enlisted men perform essentially the same chores that the strikers did during the period of the Indian Wars.

37. Testimony of Colonel Robert E. Johnston, February 15, 1876; and of Colonel Guy V. Henry, Sr., February 14, 1876. Both officers appeared before the Banning Committee on Military Affairs in Washington, D.C., U.S. Congress, House of Representatives, *The Reorganization of the Army. House Report No. 354,* 44th Cong., 1st Sess. (Washington: Government Printing Office, 1876), pp. 196, 190.

38. Merington, ed., *The Custer Story,* p. 253; Custer, *Following the Guidon,* pp. 314-315.

39. Custer, *Boots and Saddles,* p. 61.

40. Frances Carrington, *My Army Life,* p. 55; Lydia Spenser Lane, *I Married a Soldier or Old Days in the Old Army* (Philadelphia: J.B. Lippincott Company, 1893), pp. 154-155; Boyd, *Cavalry Life,* pp. 195-199; Grace Paulding, "My Army Life," pp. 12-13.

41. FitzGerald, *Army Doctor's Wife,* pp. 59-60, 172-173, 208, 230-232.

42. Roe, *Army Letters,* pp. 234, 286-287, 289.

43. Ibid., pp. 184-185.

44. Burt, "Forty Years," p. 174; Mattes, *Indians, Infants and Infantry,* p. 157; Biddle, *Reminscences,* pp. 173, 193.

45. Biddle, *Reminiscences,* p. 173; Frances Carrington, *My Army Life,* pp. 107, 105; Burt, "Forty Years," p. 92.

46. Summerhayes, *Vanished Arizona,* pp. 26-28.

47. FitzGerald, *Army Doctor's Wife,* pp. 50, 198. The *Report of the Surgeon General, 1891* mentions the case of a woman who died as a result of using clove tea as an abortifacient. War Department, *Annual Report of the Secretary of War, 1891,* 2 vols. (Washington: Government Printing Office, 1891), I, p. 607; Merington, ed., *The Custer Story,* p. 102.

48. FitzGerald, *Army Doctor's Wife,* p. 70.

49. Ibid.

50. Boyd, *Cavalry Life,* pp. 92-93; Summerhayes, *Vanished Arizona,* p. 109; Biddle, *Reminiscences,* p. 169.

51. FitzGerald, *Army Doctor's Wife,* p. 165.

52. Boyd, *Cavalry Life,* p. 141; Fougera, *With Custer's Cavalry,* pp. 167-168.

53. Fougera, *With Custer's Cavalry,* pp. 254-256; Biddle, *Reminiscences,* p. 195.

134

54. Roe, *Army Letters*, pp. 32-34.

55. Ibid., pp. 87-89. Mrs. Custer described a Texas norther as being "preceded by the unusual heavy, suffocating air which renders breathing an effort," and that is followed by the "wild blast of wind . . . of an undescribable fury." Custer, *Tenting on the Plains*, p. 115.

56. Biddle, *Reminiscences*, pp. 123-124; Colonel Benjamin H. Grierson to Mrs. Alice Grierson, October 3, 1866, The Grierson Papers. Quoted by William H. Leckie, *The Buffalo Soldiers* (Norman: University of Oklahoma Press, 1967), p. 13.

57. Roe, *Army Letters*, pp. 316-318; Boyd, *Cavalry Life*, pp. 221-222.

58. Summerhayes, *Vanished Arizona*, pp. 211, 160, 234, 184-186, 219.

59. Custer, *Tenting on the Plains*, p. 322; Roe, *Army Letters*, pp. 292-294; Fougera, *With Custer's Cavalry*, pp. 214-219.

60. Erwin N. Thompson, "The Negro Soldiers on the Frontier: A Fort Davis Case Study," *Journal of the West*, VII (April, 1968), 231-232; Custer, *Tenting on the Plains*, p. 320.

61. Burt, "Forty Years," p. 41; Custer, *Boots and Saddles*, p. 68. In this passage Mrs. Custer exposed the romantic bent of her nature.

62. FitzGerald, *Army Doctor's Wife*, pp. 249, 257.

63. Ibid., pp. 262-263, 301.

64. Everett Dick, *Vanguards of the Frontier: A Social History of the Northern Plains and Rocky Mountains* (New York: Tudor Publishing Company, 1941), p. 100; Merintgon, ed., *The Custer Story*, pp. 321-323.

65. Merington, ed., *The Custer Story*, pp. 321-323. Ms. Merington erred when she referred to the commander of Fort Abraham Lincoln as Captain McCluskey. The post commander who broke the news of the "Massacre" was Captain William Spenser McCaskey. See Colonel W.A. Graham, *The Custer Myth: A Source Book of Custeriana* (New York: Bonanaza Books, 1953), p. 282.

66. Fougera, *With Custer's Cavalry*, pp. 265-266.

67. FitzGerald, *An Army Doctor's Wife*, p. 275; Simon Snyder to his mother, Mrs. M.C. Snyder, July 30, 1876. Loaned for copying from the Snyder-Ronayne Collection, Custer Battlefield National Monument, Crow Agency, Montana. Copy available in the Don Rickey, Jr., Collection, Denver, Colorado. Captain James Porter was killed with Custer's command, and the burial parties were unable to locate his head although they identified the trunk of a body as his.

68. Merington, ed., *The Custer Story*, p. 326; Roe, *Army Letters*, p. 120.

69. William H. Glasson, *Federal Military Pensions in the United States*. Edited by David Kinley (New York: Oxford University Press, 1918), p. 115.

70. Summerhayes, *Vanished Arizona*, pp. 243-246. Mrs. Custer, however, wrote about a meeting she had with Mrs. Nelson A. Miles soon after her husband's promotion to brigadier general. Mrs. Miles missed the "men and women with whom she had suffered in the blizzards, siroccos, hurricanes, and above all the unceasing fear and anxiety about hostile Indians." In Southern California, surrounded by vineyards and roses, she longed for the "bleak wastes of Dakota." See Custer, *Following the Guidon*, pp. 280-281.

71. Biddle, *Reminiscences*, pp. 167-168.

72. Roe, *Army Letters*, p. 216. Mrs. Roe related that the enlisted men

did not lack sources of entertainment. "Every morning there are drills and a funny kind of target practice inside the quarters, and of course there are inspections and other things." Ibid., p. 222.

73. Ibid., pp. 185-190.

74. Mary Rippley Heistand, "Scraps from an Army Woman's Diary: An Old Army Christmas," *Army and Navy Life,* IX (December, 1907), 626-631.

75. Fougera, *With Custer's Cavalry,* pp. 190-192; Custer, *Boots and Saddles,* p. 115.

76. Roe, *Army Letters,* pp. 231-232; Biddle, *Reminiscences* p. 65; Boyd, *Cavalry Life,* p. 260.

77. Margaret Carrington, *Ab-Sa-Ra-Ka, Land of Massacre,* p. 177; Frances Carrington, *My Army Life,* p. 102; Roe, *Army Letters,* p. 222; FitzGerald, *Army Doctor's Wife,* p. 228; Dale Frederick Giese, "Social Life at Fort Union, New Mexico in the 1880's," (Unpublished Master's thesis, New Mexico Highlands University, 1964), pp. 120, 122.

78. Boyd, *Cavalry Life,* p. 238; Roe, *Army Letters,* pp. 363-364.

79. Biddle, *Reminiscences,* p. 86; Roe, *Army Letters,* pp. 268-269; Fougera, *With Custer's Cavalry,* pp. 151-155. Rufus Zogbaum wrote that some of the women living on one western post joined the men in target practice. He referred to the ladies as "no mean shots." Rufus F. Zogbaum, *Horses, Foot, and Dragoons: Sketches of Army Life at Home and Abroad* (New York: Harper and Brothers, 1888), p. 162.

80. Boyd, *Cavalry Life,* p. 69; Roe, *Army Letters,* pp. 298-299.

81. Fougera, *With Custer's Cavalry,* p. 134; Merington, ed., *The Custer Story,* p. 270; Custer, *Boots and Saddles,* pp. 133-134; Burt, "Forty Years," p. 204; Boyd, *Cavalry Life,* pp. 288-290. At Fort Concho, Texas, in 1877, the Constables entertained officers' row by purchasing a new "cottage piano." Some residents of the post were less than appreciative of Mrs. Constable's playing. Susan Miles, *Fort Concho in 1877* (San Angelo, Texas: The Bradley Company, 1972), p. 39.

82. Margaret Carrington, *Ab-Sa-Ra-Ka, Land of Massacre,* pp. 178-179; Summerhayes, *Vanished Arizona,* pp. 221-222; Reynolds J. Burt, "Boyhood Data, 1874-1890." Don Rickey, Jr., Collection, Denver, Colorado, p. 12; Burt, "Forty Years," p. 110; FitzGerald, *Army Doctor's Wife,* p. 218.

83. Giese, "Social History of Fort Union," p. 12; Lane, *I Married a Soldier,* p. 164; Chaplain George W. Dunbar's daughter Alice played the organ for her father's church services at Fort Concho. Miles, *Fort Concho in 1877,* p. 29.

84. Roe, *Army Letters,* pp. 338-341.

85. Ibid., p. 166.

Chapter 3
ENLISTED MEN'S WIVES, LAUNDRESSES, and "CAMP FOLLOWERS"

1. Major Gerald E. Griffin, *Ballads of the Regiment* (New York: George U. Harvey Publishing Company, 1918), p. 30.

2. S.E. Whitman, *The Troopers: An Informal History of the Plains Cavalry, 1865-1890* (New York: Hastings House, 1962), p. 145; Raymond Leo Welty, "The Western Army Frontier, 1860-1870," (Unpublished Ph.D. thesis, State University of Iowa, 1924), pp. 347-348.

3. Adjutant General's Office, General Orders No. 140, *Index of General Orders, 1861* (Washington: Government Printing Office, 1862).

4. War Department, *Revised United States Regulations of 1861* (Washington: Government Printing Office, 1863), p. 130.

5. War Department, *Regulations of the Army of the United States, 1901* (Washington: Government Printing Office, 1902), p. 127; James A. Moss, *Officers' Manual (For use of subalterns)* (Menosha, Wisconsin: Press of the George Banta Publishing Company, 1907), p. 176.

6. Johnny O'Brien, Interview, April 4, 1961. Typescript of this interview conducted at Fort Laramie by Jack McDermott, Rex Wilson, and Sally Johnson is available in the U.S. Army Military History Institute, U.S. Army War College, Carlisle Barracks, Pennsylvania; Custer, *Boots and Saddles*, p. 95.

7. Colonel John E. Smith to H.B. Banning, Chairman of the House Military Committee, February 16, 1876. This letter is part of the evidence offered in *The Reorganization of the Army, House Report No. 354*, 44th Cong., 1st Sess. (Washington: Government Printing Office, 1876), p. 102.

8. Roy P. Johnson, "Jacob Horner of the 7th Cavalry," *North Dakota History*, XVI (April, 1949), pp. 77, 97-98.

9. *Medical History of Camp Supply, 1879*, Vol. 168, Record Group 94, National Archives, p. 211; Surgeon General's Office, *Circular No. 4, A Report of Barracks and Hospitals with Descriptions of Military Posts, 1870* (Washington: Government Printing Office, 1870), p. 265; Surgeon General's Office, *Circular No. 8, A Report of the Hygiene of the United States Army with Descriptions of Military Posts* (Washington: Government Printing Office, 1875), pp. 254, 279.

10. Surgeon General's Office, *Circular No. 8*, 1875, pp. 545, 562.

11. Ibid., *Circular No. 4*, 1870, p. 280.

12. Adjutant General's Office, Circular No. 6, *General Orders, Circulars and General Court-Martial Orders, 1883* (Washington: Government Printing Office, 1884); Ibid., Circular No. 8 (September 6, 1887), *General Orders, Circulars, and General Court-Martial Orders, 1887* (Washington: Government Printing Office, 1888).

13. Lieutenant General William T. Sherman to Committee on Military Affairs, Febraury 4, 1878. This letter was entered as part of the record in *Reorganization of the Army: Report of a Sub-committee of the Committee on Military Affairs Relating to the Reorganization of the Army, House Miscellaneous Document No. 56*, 45th Cong., 2nd Sess. (Washington: Government Printing Office, 1878), p. 8.

14. Alice Mathews Shields, "Army Life on the Wyoming Frontier," *Annals of Wyoming*, XIII (October, 1941), pp. 332-337.

15. James M. Merrill, *Spurs to Glory: The Story of the United States Cavalry* (New York: Rand McNally and Company, 1966), pp. 185-186.

16. Custer, *Following the Guidon*, pp. 12-13.

17. *Report of the Secretary of War*, 1891, I, p. 605; *Medical History of Fort Stockton, May, 1869-October, 1872*, Vol. 63, Record Group 94,

National Archives, p. 13. In 1891, the *Report of the Secretary of War* listed 14,450 civilians associated with the United States Army.

18. Wilbur S. Nye, *Carbine and Lance: The Story of Old Fort Sill* (Norman: University of Oklahoma Press, 1937), pp. 360-361; Whitman, *The Troopers*, p. 145.

19. Testimony of Inspector General R.B. Marcy, January 1, 1878, *Reorganization of the Army, House Miscellaneous Document No. 56*, 45th Cong., 2nd Sess., pp. 50-51; Testimony of Captain Henry G. Thomas, February 26, 1876, *The Reorganization of the Army, House Report No. 354*, 44th Cong., 1st Sess., p. 204.

20. Testimony of Captain Henry G. Thomas, *House Report No. 354*, 44th Cong., 1st Sess., p. 204. For the right of company laundresses to requisition rations, see Orders No. 94, *Post Order Book*, Headquarters of the Sixth Infantry, Fort Atkinson, April 6, 1824, pp. 69-70.

21. *American State Papers, 1789-1838*, 38 vols. (Washington: Gales and Seaton, 1832-1861), *Military Affairs*, II, No. 199, pp. 211, 217. The post Council of Administration was composed of the commanding officer, the three individuals next in rank to him, a fourth officer to act as a secretary, and the post sutler. This group met every two months. Fort Boise, *Letters Received, 1864-1867*, Record Group No. 393, National Archives.

22. Nye, *Carbine and Lance*, p. 360; Surgeon General's Office, *Circular No. 8*, 1875, p. 233.

23. Sixth Infantry Orders, Fort Atkinson, October 8, 1923 to October, 1824, p. 180.

24. Mrs. McCormack to Major L.H. Marshall, June 9, 1866. This letter is offered for sale by Don's Military Outpost, P.O. Box 63, Boston, Massachusetts.

25. Captain Eugene F. Ware, *The Indian War of 1864* (Lincoln: University of Nebraska Press, 1965), pp. 123-126.

26. Custer, *Boots and Saddles*, pp. 188-192; Rickey, *Forty Miles a Day on Beans and Hay*, pp. 170-171; Fougera, *With Custer's Cavalry*, pp. 222-223. The corporal reportedly committed suicide.

27. Custer, *Boots and Saddles*, p. 189.

28. Ibid., p. 191; FitzGerald, *Army Doctor's Wife*, p. 50; Report of General J.C. Kelton to Henry Banning, Chairman of the House Committee on Military Affairs, February 15, 1876. This report is contained in *The Reorganization of the Army, House Report No. 354*, 44th Cong., 1st Sess., p. 131.

29. Ami Frank Mulford, *Fighting Indians in the 7th United States Cavalry* (Corning, New York: Paul Lindsley Mulford, 1879), p. 52.

30. Custer, *Tenting on the Plains*, p. 263.

31. Nye, *Carbine and Lance*, pp. 360-361; Whitman, *The Troopers*, p. 145; Merrill, *Spurs to Glory*, p. 178.

32. Brigadier General George A. Forsyth, *The Story of the Soldier*, Vol. 1, *Builders of the Nation* (New York: D. Appleton and Company, 1900), pp. 132-133.

33. The evidence gathered by the Banning Committee and the committee of 1878 led to many changes in the structure of the army, not the least of which was the abolition of the position of company laundress. Colonel Robert E. Johnston was one of the officers who believed that it

would be a great injustice to discharge the "old soldier-laundresses."

34. Report of General George Sykes to the Banning Committee, February 10, 1876, *House Report No. 354,* 1876, p. 106; Report of General J.C. Kelton to the Banning Committee, February 15, 1876, *House Report No. 354,* 1876, pp. 130-131.

35. Testimony of General E.O.C. Ord before the Banning Committee, *House Report No. 354,* 1876, p. 46.

36. Report of Colonel Philippe Régis de Trobriand, February 12, 1876, *House Report No. 354,* 1876, pp. 98-99. Colonel de Trobriand had not always thought that women did not belong on the frontier. In 1868, he had expressed his great admiration for the officers' wives who had braved extreme hardships to be with their husbands. Philippe Régis Denis de Keredern, Comte de Trobriand, *Vie Militaire dans le Dakota: Notes et Souvenirs, 1867-1869* (Paris: Librarie Ancienne, Honore Champion, 1926), pp. 233-234.

37. Report of Lieutenant Colonel R.I. Dodge to the Banning Committee, February 10, 1876, *House Report No. 354,* 1876, p. 120; Testimony of Captain Henry G. Thomas before the Banning Committee, February 26, 1876, *House Report No. 354,* 1876, pp. 201-204.

38. Lieutenant Colonel O.H. Hein, *Memories of Long Ago* (New York: G.P. Putnam's Sons, 1925), pp. 67-68; Marian Russell, *Land of Enchantment: Memoirs of Marian Russell Along the Santa Fé Trail.* Dictated to Mrs. Hal Russell. Edited by Garnet M. Bayer (Evanston, Illinois: The Branding Iron Press, 1954), p. 110.

39. Whitman, *The Troopers,* p. 145. One example of this is the testimony of Inspector General R.B. Marcy on January 1, 1878, before the House Committee on Military Affairs. *House Miscellaneous Document No. 56,* 45th Cong., 2nd Sess., 1878, pp. 50-51.

40. Adjutant General's Office, General Orders No. 37, *Index of General Orders, 1878* (Washington: Government Printing Office, 1879), p. 8.

41. Special Orders No. 122, *Post and Regimental Order Book,* Fort Totten, Headquarters, 7th Cavalry, January 1878-December, 1881, p. 155; Circular No. 17, *Post Order Book,* Fort Meade, January, 1887-November, 1887, p. 27.

42. Mulford, *Fighting Indians,* p. 60. Mulford described the officers' ladies as "painted dolls."

43. Welty, "Western Army Frontier, 1860-1870," p. 348.

44. Custer, *Boots and Saddles,* p. 133; Biddle, *Reminiscences,* pp. 175-176; Mattes, *Indians, Infants and Infantry,* pp. 97, 179.

45. Frances Carrington, *My Army Life,* pp. 199-200. Mrs. Carrington wrote that the soldiers whose wives worked as company laundresses "regulated their domestic discipline aside from fixed methods and punished their wives sternly for indecent bossing."

46. FitzGerald, *Army Doctor's Wife,* pp. 59-60, 172-173.

47. Ibid., *Army Doctor's Wife,* pp. 286-287.

48. Custer, *Boots and Saddles,* pp. 94-96. Mrs. Custer confided that the general expressed a fear that she would show her tactlessness and laugh at the women's dancing costumes.

49. Ibid., p. 96; Ibid., *Following the Guidon,* p. 55.

50. Jake Tonamichel to Don Rickey, Jr., March 13, 1957. This letter is part of the Don Rickey, Jr., Collection, Denver, Colorado; Maurice Frink

and Casey Barthelmess, *Photographer on an Army Mule* (Norman: University of Oklahoma Press, 1965), pp. 94-95.

51. Statement of General E.O.C. Ord before the Banning Committee, February 17, 1876, *House Report No. 354,* 1876, p. 43.

52. Ray H. Mattison, "The Army Posts on the Northern Plains, 1865-1885," *Nebraska History,* XXXV (March, 1954), 30. The most common diseases at these posts were of the respiratory and intestinal organs, and rheumatism.

53. Rickey, *Forty Miles a Day on Beans and Hay,* p. 131. For statistical information concerning the prevalence of venereal diseases in the United States Army, see the *Surgeon General's Report, Annual Report of the Secretary of War, 1891,* I, pp. 593-681.

54. Sergeant Reginald A. Bradley, Interview, Grass Valley, California, January 10, 1968. This interview was conducted by Don Rickey, Jr., for the National Park Service. A typescript of it is available in the Don Rickey, Jr., Collection, Denver, Colorado; Rickey, *Forty Miles a Day on Beans and Hay,* p. 170. Private John G. Ford, who reported that a "few accomodating women" accompanied his unit on march, stated that each morning the doctor examined the men who had relations with the women.

55. Adjutant General's Office, General Orders No. 24, *Index of General Orders, 1881* (Washington: Government Printing Office, 1882).

56. John Dishon McDermott, "Crime and Punishment in the United States Army: A Phase of Fort Laramie History," *Journal of the West,* VII (April, 1968), p. 246; Jake Tonamichel to Don Rickey, Jr., March 17, 1957. This letter is part of the Don Rickey, Jr., Collection, Denver, Colorado; Forsyth, *The Soldier,* pp. 140-141.

57. Custer, *Boots and Saddles,* pp. 218-219.

58. Chris Emmett, *Fort Union and the Winning of the Southwest* (Norman: University of Oklahoma Press, 1964), pp. 141-144; Giese, "Social Life at Fort Union," pp. 169-170. At his court-martial, Captain Sykes, in a "fervid oral defense," established to the satisfaction of the court that he was not guilty of conduct unbecoming a gentleman.

59. Emmett, *Fort Union,* pp. 323-324.

60. Erwin N. Thompson, "The Negro Soldiers on the Frontier: A Fort Davis Case Sudy," *Journal of the West,* VII (April, 1968), 232.

61. Johnny O'Brien, Interview, April 4, 1961.

62. Rickey, *Forty Miles a Day on Beans and Hay,* p. 168; Colonel William Paulding, "A Few Words on My Army Life, from 1874 to 1913," The Grace and William Paulding Papers, U.S. Army Military History Institute, U.S. Army War College, Carlisle Barracks, Pennsylvania, p. 23.

63. Ray H. Mattison, ed., "The Diary of Surgeon Washington Mathews," *North Dakota History,* XXI (January-April, 1954), 19. Local authorities made no efforts to drive the prostitutes out of town or close their houses in the small community known as The Flat which grew up outside Fort Griffin, Texas. Instead, during the 1870s and 1880s, the madams were arraigned before the Justice's court annually and fined one hundred dollars for running disorderly houses. After they paid their fines, they were free from arrest for another year unless they committed other kinds of offenses. Carl Coke Rister, *Fort Griffin on the Texas Frontier* (Norman: University of Oklahoma Press, 1956), pp. 134-135.

Chapter 4
GROWING UP ON THE PLAINS

1. Reynolds J. Burt, "Boyhood Data, 1874-1890," p. 23.
2. Phillipe Régis de Trobriand, *Army Life in Dakota.* Edited by Milo Quaife. Translated by George F. Will (Chicago: Lakeside Press, 1941), p. 41.
3. Custer, *Boots and Saddles,* p. 119.
4. La Guardia, *The Making of an Insurgent,* p. 19; Guy V. Henry, Jr., "A Brief Life of Guy V. Henry, Jr.," U.S. Army Military History Institute, U.S. Army War College, Carlisle Barracks, Pennsylvania, p. 6.
5. Merrill, *Spurs to Glory,* p. 186. In 1891, one hundred and forty-one out of 6,163 children attached to the army succumbed to infantile diseases and fatal injuries. *Report of the Surgeon General, Annual Report of the Secretary of War, 1891,* I, p. 605.
6. *Medical History of Camp Supply,* 1877, Vol. 168, RG 94, NA, pp. 124, 141, 150.
7. Mattes, *Indians, Infants and Infantry,* p. 232; *Medical History of Camp Supply, 1879,* Vol. 168, p. 244. Only one of the vaccinations given the children at Camp Supply was effective. Camp Supply, established in November, 1868, was situated between the Northern Canadian River and Wolf Creek in Indian Territory. The camp became a fort in 1878. Robert W. Frazer, *Forts of the West* (Norman: University of Oklahoma Press, 1965), p. 124. In this work, Frazer describes each of the forts mentioned in this work.
8. Boyd, *Cavalry Life,* pp. 298-299. Mrs. Boyd did not give her children's names. For a brief summary of the career of Captain Boyd and the other officers noted in this work, see Francis B. Heitman, *Historical Record and Dictionary of the United States Army from 1789 to 1903,* 2 vols. (Washington: Government Printing Office, 1903).
9. Henry, Jr., "Brief Life," pp. 2-6. For a description of Fort Sill in 1870, see Surgeon General's Office, *Circular No. 4,* 1870, p. 265.
10. Henry, Jr., "Brief Life," pp. 6, 12.
11. Captain Snyder somewhat laconically commented in his diary entry for October 5, 1869: "For fear of forgetting it I record that May and I were married today." Diaries of Captain Simon Snyder from 1866 through the 1880's. Loaned for copying by the Custer Battlefield National Monument, Crow Agency, Montana. Copied by Don Rickey, Jr., and placed in the U.S. Army Military History Institute, U.S. Army War College, Carlisle Barracks, Pennsylvania.
12. Captain Simon Snyder to his mother, Mrs. M.C. Snyder, September 19, 1876, p. 3. All letters of Captain Snyder cited in this paper were loaned for copying from the Snyder-Ronayne Collection, Custer Battlefield Monument, Crow Agency, Montana. Copy available in the Don Rickey, Jr., Collection, Denver, Colorado.
13. Snyder, Diary, July 16, 1877.
14. Snyder, Diary, December 26, 1880, January 2, 1881. Once an officer died, his family could no longer exercise any legal claim to government housing and were expected to vacate the quarters as soon as possible.

Even Mrs. Elizabeth Custer felt compelled to surrender her quarters at Fort Abraham Lincoln very soon after the events of July 25, 1876, became known. Merington, ed., *The Custer Story,* p. 326.

15. A fitting postscript is that Lillie Snyder married an enlisted man who later became an officer. Lillie's daughter Dorothy Ronayne lives in San Antonio, Texas.

16. Henry, Jr., "Brief Life," pp. 3-7. For an account of the military exploits of Guy V. Henry, Sr., see "On Their Battle Banner: Frail Captain Henry Fought Sioux in 1876 and Refused to Die," *New York World Telegram,* Saturday, September 30, 1939, Sec. II, p. 19.

17. Frederick W. Sladen, "Childhood and Early Career Correspondences, 1874-1916," Item from around April, 1880, Sladen Family Papers, U.S. Army Military History Institute, U.S. Army War College, Carlisle Barracks, Pennsylvania.

18. Margaret Carrington, *Ab-Sa-Ra-Ka, Land of Massacre,* p. 52; Henry, Jr., "Brief Life," p. 11. Saidee Henry later married Lieutenant James Benton who died in a swimming accident at Hot Springs, South Dakota in 1896. Biddle, *Reminiscences,* pp. 231-233.

19. La Guardia, *The Making of an Insurgent,* p. 19; James H. Van Horn, "The Frontier Army's Environment," (Unpublished manuscript in the possession of Don Rickey, Jr., Denver, Colorado), pp. 204-206, 216. General Douglas MacArthur, who grew up on the western military frontier, recalled that he learned to ride and to shoot before he could read or write — "indeed almost before I could walk and talk." General Douglas MacArthur, *Reminiscences* (New York: McGraw-Hill Book Company, 1964), p. 15.

20. Fred Sladen to his father, First Lieutenant Joseph A. Sladen, April 4, 1880, "Childhood and Early Career Correspondences, 1874-1916."

21. Boyd, *Cavalry Life,* p. 267; Van Horn, "Frontier Army," p. 204.

22. "Brigadier General Andrew S. Burt was the first commissioned officer to step over the line and play baseball with his men." Excerpt from the *Daily Missoulin,* April 30, 1907, quoted by Mattes, *Indians, Infants and Infantry,* p. 266; Burt, "Boyhood Data," p. 41.

23. Johnny O'Brien, Interview, April 4, 1961; Burt, "Boyhood Data," pp. 31, 41. Euchre, a card game played by two to four participants, utilizes a thirty-two-card deck, with all the cards below seven discarded except the four aces.

24. Snyder, Diary, January 24, 1880; Ibid., July 18, 1887.

25. Snyder, Diary, Christmas Day, 1879.

26. FitzGerald, *Army Doctor's Wife,* pp. 320-321.

27. Fred Sladen to his father, First Lieutenant J.A. Sladen, December 9, 1880; Burt, "Boyhood Data," p. 12; Fourgera, *With Custer's Cavalry,* pp. 239-244.

28. Snyder, Diary, July 4, 1878; Van Horn, "Frontier Army," p. 217; Fred Sladen to his father, First Lieutenant J.A. Sladen, March 30, 1875.

29. Fred Sladen to his father, First Lieutenant J.A. Sladen, March 21, 1880; La Guardia, *The Making of an Insurgent,* p. 20; Burt, "Boyhood Data," p. 13.

30. Biddle, *Reminiscences,* pp. 102-104.

31. Mattes, *Indians, Infants and Infantry,* pp. 200-202.

32. Captain Snyder recorded in his diary on July 23, 1878: "Mosquitoes very bad last night, so did not sleep much, most of my time being occupied in keeping the pests off Lillie."

33. Burt, "Boyhood Data," pp. 22-23.

34. Captain John G. Bourke, "Bourke on the Southwest." Edited by Lansing Bloom, *New Mexico Historical Review,* IX (April, 1934), 183; James F. Walker, "Old Fort Berthold as I Knew It," *North Dakota History,* XX (January, 1953), 34-35.

35. Jake Tonamichel to Don Rickey, Jr., March 13, 1957, Don Rickey, Jr., Collection, Denver, Colorado; La Guardia, *The Making of an Insurgent,* p. 20.

36. Custer, *Following the Guidon,* p. 310.

37. Henry, Jr., "A Brief Life," p. 3; Fred Sladen to his father, First Lieutenant J.A. Sladen, December 9, 1880.

38. Burt, "Boyhood Data," pp. 2, 5; Summerhayes, *Vanished Arizona,* p. 261.

39. Rickey, *Forty Miles a Day on Beans and Hay,* p. 194.

40. *Regulations of the Army of the United States and the General Orders in Force on the 17th of February, 1881.* Published by order of the Secretary of War (Washington: Government Printing Office, 1881), p. 57.

41. Ibid. For the appearance of school children at Fort Davis, Texas, in 1883, see Mrs. M.B. Anderson, "A School is Started in Old Fort Davis," *Women Tell the Story of the Southwest.* Compiled and edited by Mattie L. Wooten (San Antonio, Texas: The Naylor Company, 1940), p. 298.

42. *Regulations, 1881,* p. 57.

43. Ibid., pp. 57-58.

44. O'Brien Interview, April 4, 1961; Jake Tonamichel to Don Rickey, Jr., March 13, 1957.

45. Henry, Jr., "Brief Life," p. 12.

46. Fred Sladen to his father, First Lieutenant J.A. Sladen, February 29, 1880.

47. Captain John G. Bourke, "Bourke on the Southwest." Edited by Lansing Bloom, *New Mexico Historical Review,* IX, 279-280.

48. Henry, Jr., "Brief Life," p. 5; MacArthur, *Reminiscences,* p. 16; Van Horn, "Frontier Army," p. 220. MacArthur related that his mother took the responsibility for his early education. Among other precepts, she taught him a sense of obligation and that his country was always to come first. He must not do two things: "Never lie, never tattle."

49. Snyder observed Lillie's going away by confiding to his diary on August 29, 1887: "The dear little girl bears up most heroically under the strain of excitement upon leaving . . . for a year . . . May God bless and protect her."

50. Henry, Jr., "Brief Life," p. 10; Mattes, *Indians, Infants and Infantry,* p. 256; Biddle, *Reminiscences,* pp. 139-141; Boyd, *Cavalry Life,* p. 299.

51. Leckie, *The Buffalo Soldiers,* p. 71; Colonel William S. Paulding, "My Army Life," The William and Grace Paulding Papers, U.S. Army Military History Institute, U.S. Army War College, Carlisle Barracks, Pennsylvania, p. 57.

Chapter 5
MEN AND WOMEN

1. Speech in summation delivered by Judge Advocate Major Thomas F. Barr, Major Marcus A. Reno General Court-Martial (1877), Record Group 153, QQ 87, Drawer 60, National Archives, p. 34.

2. Fougera, *With Custer's Cavalry*, p. 74; Downey, *Indian-Fighting Army*, p. 110.

3. Merington (editor), *The Custer Story*, p. 194; Custer, *Boots and Saddles*, pp. 130-132. See also Mary Julia Allen to Mrs. Carrie Riker, March 5, 1868. The letters of Lt. Colonel and Mrs. H.A. Allen, as compiled by Mrs. Victor R. Evans, are on file at San Juan Island National Historical Site, Friday Harbor, Washington and used by permission of Ms. Patricia Milliren, Historian. The Allen letters offer another valuable source of information about the lives of army dependents on the Pacific Coastal frontier during the period of the Indian Wars.

4. Bourke, "Bourke on the Southwest," Edited by Lansing Bloom, *New Mexico Historical Review*, X (January, 1935), 25. President Grant evened the score the next time he met Mrs. Crook. When she asked if the president really expected her to travel through Indian country to rejoin her husband, he replied quite seriously, "No, I am going to send General Crook to Alaska and you can join him at San Francisco." General Crook, contrary to his popular image, was susceptible to the charms of attractive and intelligent women who "could prevail with him where the most eloquent advocate or learned logician would utterly fail." Major A.H. Nickerson, "Major General George Crook and the Indians: A Sketch," The Crook-Kennon Papers, U.S. Army Military History Research Collection, U.S. Army War College, Carlisle Barracks, Pennsylvania, p. 31. On April 1, 1977 the name of the Research Collection changed to the U.S. Army Military History Institute.

5. Paulding, "A Few Words on My Army Life," pp. 21-22. Mrs. Custer also wrote that it was her good fortune never to encounter one of these "female grenadiers."

6. Bourke, "Bourke on the Southwest," *New Mexico Historical Review*, IX, 50. The act of 1869 which reorganized the U.S. Army on a peacetime basis created a special review board which evaluated the qualifications and performance of individual officers. Those found unfit or unqualified by the board were retired with a year's pay.

7. Roe, *Army Letters*, p. 82.

8. Frances C. Carrington, *My Army Life*, pp. 208-209. Annie Blanche Sokalski seemed to enjoy her life as a cavalry officer's wife because she loved to ride and was skilled with her husband's pistols and rifle. Eventually she acquired two colts of her own which she wore in holsters strapped low on her hips.

9. Adjutant General's Office, General Court-Martial Orders, No. 177 (July 10, 1866), *Index of General Court-Martial Orders, 1866* (Washington: Government Printing Office, 1867), pp. 1-3.

10. Testimony of Captain Tenedor Ten Eyck, Sokalski General Court-

Martial (1866), Record Group 153, MM 3975, Box 891, National Archives, p. 15.

11. Examination of Lieutenant Seneca H. Norton, Sokalski Court-Martial proceedings. Sokalski GCM, RG 153, MM 3975, Box 891, NA, p. 59. Lieutenant Norton's remarks have a curiously modern sound.

12. General Court-Martial Orders No. 177 (1866), pp. 4-5.

13. See the letter from Captain Sokalski to the Judge Advocate in which the accused explained the necessity of his wife's appearing before the court, and the Sokalski GCM, p. 57.

14. For the full list of charges and specifications brought against Captain Sokalski, see General Court-Martial Orders No. 177 (1866), pp. 1-7; Brown, *Gentle Tamers,* p. 65.

15. Testimony of Lieutenant Norton, Sokalski GCM, RG 153, MM 3975, Bx 891, NA, pp. 25-26.

16. Bruce J. Dinges, "The Court-Martial of Lieutenant Henry O. Flipper: An Example of Black-White Relationships in the Army, 1881," *The American West,* IX (January, 1972), 12-13. Flipper was a rare exception – a black officer in the 10th Cavalry. According to the law creating both the 9th and 10th Cavalries, no blacks were to be elevated past the rank of sergeant. All officers were to be white men.

17. Dinges, "Court-Martial of Lieutenant Flipper," *The American West,* IX, 13-14; Leckie, *The Buffalo Soldiers,* p. 238.

18. General Court-Martial of Lieutenant Henry Flipper (June, 1882), Record Group 153, QQ 2952, Boxes 2032, 2033, National Archives, p. 78.

19. Testimony of Lucy E. Smith, Flipper GCM, RG 153, QQ 2952, Bx 2032-2033, NA, p. 462.

20. Testimony of Colonel William R. Shafter, Flipper GCM, RG 153, QQ 2952, Bx 2032-2033, NA, p. 84.

21. This point was made by Captain Barber in his summation. See Dinges, "Court-Martial of Lieutenant Flipper," *The American West,* IX, 60. In recent years many influential members of the black community joined military historians in an attempt to clear Flipper's name. On December 13, 1976, Assistant Secretary of the Army Donald G. Brotzman ordered the Army Board for Corrections of Military Records to correct army records to show that Flipper was separated on a certificate of honorable discharge on June 30, 1882.

22. General Court-Martial of Private Andy Clayton, Company H, 9th Cavalry convened at Fort Sill, Indian Territory, May 21, 1874. Record Group 153, PP 3995, National Archives, p. 5.

23. Ibid., p. 8-9.

24; For the complete list of charges and specifications against Captain French, see Adjutant General's Office, General Court-Martial Orders, No. 19 (March 26, 1879), *Index of General Court-Martial Orders* (Washington: Government Printing Office, 1880), pp. 1-3.

25. Ibid., p. 4.

26. From Brigadier General A.H. Terry, Commander of the Department of Dakota, to General W.T. Sherman, General of the Army. This letter is located in the French GCM, RG 153, QQ 994, Bx 1902, National Archives.

27. General Philip H. Sheridan to President Grover Cleveland, April 8, 1887. This letter contains references to Major Benteen's past military

record and the recommendation that the sentence be entirely remitted. Benteen General Court-Martial (1887), Record Group 153, RR 2327, Box 2271, National Archives.

28. Testimony of Captain J.A. Olmstead, Benteen GCM, RG 153, RR 2327, Bx 2271, NA, pp. 17-18.

29. Testimony of Miss Violet Norman, Benteen GCM, RG 153, RR 2327, Bx 2271, NA, pp. 151-152. For the complete list of charges and specifications brought against Major Benteen, see Adjutant General's Office, General Court-Martial Orders, No. 34, *Index of General Court-Martial Orders, 1887* (Washington: Government Printing Office, 1888), pp. 1-2.

30. Several officers including Captains E.S. Godfrey and F.M. Gibson wrote a joint-letter to President Cleveland and asked that he show mercy to the man they credited with saving their lives at the Battle of the Little Big Horn. This letter is included in the Benteen General Court-Martial proceedings of 1887.

31. Testimony of Doctor C. Carlos Carvallo in the Colonel N.A.M. Dudley General Court-Martial (1877), Record Group 153, QQ 448, Drawer 61, Box 1886, National Archives, p. 82; Emmett, *Fort Union,* p. 380. There were three types of courts-martial: regimental and garrison, in which enlisted men were tried for less serious offenses, and general courts-martial which were convened by department commanders and which judged enlisted men accused of more serious crimes and officers charged with any offense. See Robert M. Utley, *Frontier Regulars: The United States Army and the Indian, 1866-1890* (New York: Macmillan Publishing Company, 1973), p. 87.

32. Emmett, *Fort Union,* p. 380; Leckie, *Buffalo Soldiers,* p. 182.

33. From Miss Lizzie Simpson to Dr. W.R. Tipton, July 23, 1877. This letter forms the body of the affidavit which Miss Simpson delivered to Colonel Dudley. Exhibit No. 23, Dudley GCM, RG 153, QQ 448, Drawer 61, Bx 1886, NA, pp. 1-3.

34. Emmett, *Fort Union,* pp. 380-381.

35. Ibid.

36. Testimony of Dr. W.R. Tipton in the Dudley GCM, RG 153, QQ 448, Drawer 61, Bx 1866, NA, pp. 94-96; Ibid., Testimony of Enoch Tipton, p. 98.

37. Ibid., Testimony of Dr. Carlos Carvallo, p. 81. In a preliminary interrogation of various subpoened witnesses, Judge Advocate Captain W.S. Tremaine threatened Lieutenant D.H. Clark with court-martial if he refused to answer certain questions. Captain Tremaine then asked Clark, "Didn't you —— that girl [Miss Simpson] yourself?" Lieutenant Clark refused to answer. However, Dr. Tipton's letters to Miss Simpson show that he was jealous of the relationship between Miss Lizzie and Clark.

38. Ibid., Testimony of Enoch Tipton, p. 99.

39. General Court-Martial Orders No. 1, Assistant-Adjutant General's Office, Headquarters, Department of the Missouri, Fort Leavenworth, Kansas, January 17, 1878, pp. 3-5.

40. Major Marcus A. Reno General Court-Martial (1877), Record Group 153, QQ 87, Drawer 60, National Archives, pp. 4-5. Reno's point of view is contained in John Upton Terrell and Colonel George Walton's *Faint the Trumpet Sounds: The Life and Trial of Major Reno* (New York: David

146

McKay Company, 1966), pp. 207-227. Reno's wife had been dead for a few years at the time of his first court-martial.

41. Reno GCM (1877), RG 153, QQ 87, Drawer 60, NA, p. 7.

42. Summation of Judge Advocate Thomas H. Barr, Reno GCM (1877), RG 153, QQ 87, Drawer 60, NA, p. 31.

43. Ibid., pp. 7-8.

44. Ibid.

45. Ibid.

46. Reno GCM (1877), RG 153, QQ 87, Drawer 60, NA, p. 10.

47. Ibid., Testimony of Captain Frederick Benteen, pp. 208-209; Testimony of Lieutenant George D. Wallace, pp. 207-208.

48. Counsel for the Defense, Reno GCM (1877), RG 153, QQ 87, DR 60, NA, pp. 260-261.

49. Ibid., Testimony of Lieutenant George D. Wallace, pp. 275-276; Testimony of Major Lewis Merrill, pp. 287-288.

50 Summation of Judge Advocate Thomas H. Barr, Reno GCM (1877), RG 153, QQ 87, DR 60, NA, pp. 33-34.

51. Ibid.

52. Adjutant General's Office, General Court-Martial Orders, No. 41 (May 10, 1877), *Index of General Court-Martial Orders* (Washington: Government Printing Office, 1878), p. 5.

53. Adjutant General's Office, General Court-Martial Orders, No. 20 (March 17, 1880), *Index of General Court-Martial Orders* (Washington: Government Printing Office, 1881), p. 2. For Reno's defense in this action, see Terrell and Walton, *Faint the Trumpet Sounds*, pp. 281-297.

54. Testimony of Colonel S.D. Sturgis in the Major Marcus A. Reno General Court-Martial (1880), Record Group 153, QQ 1554, Box 889, National Archives, p. 64.

55. Ibid., Testimony of Miss Ella Sturgis, pp. 76-77.

56. Ibid., Testimony of Major Marcus A. Reno, pp. 89-91; Testimony of Captain Frederick Benteen, p. 105.

57. Adjutant General's Office, General Court-Martial Orders, No. 20 (March 17, 1880), *Index of General Court-Martial Orders, 1880* (Washington, Government Printing Office, 1881), p. 3. On May 31, 1867, Under Secretary of the Army David E. McGiffert, in accordance with the findings of the Army Board for Correction of Military Records, directed that all Department of Army records show that Major Marcus A. Reno was honorably discharged in the grade of major on April 1, 1880.

58. Since this case is not to my knowlege part of the public record, I have chosen to change the surname of the young lady involved. For those who wish to know the full details, the Geddes Court-Martial is available at the National Archives; and for those who see this act as female chauvinism, I can only state that had the injured party been male, his surname would have been disguised also. Miss Lillie Orleans was only eighteen and a-half-hears old in 1878 when she joined her father at Fort Stockton and became infatuated with Captain Andrew Geddes of the 25th Infantry.

59. This list of charges and specifications are included in the report of Judge Advocate General Thomas M. Dunn which he submitted to George W. McCrory, Secretary of War. This report is included in the General Court-Martial of Captain Andrew Geddes (1879), Record Group 153, QQ 1387,

Box 1927, National Archives, [pages unnumbered].

60. Testimony of Miss Lillie Orleans, Geddes GCM (1879), RG 153, QQ 1387, Bx 1927, NA, pp. 29-30.

61. Ibid., pp. 34-35, 130.

62. Ibid., p. 39.

63. Ibid., p. 39.

64. Ibid., p. 41.

65. Ibid., p. 43.

66. Testimony of Captain Andrew Geddes in his own defense, Geddes GCM (1879), RG 153, QQ 1387, Bx 1927, NA, p. 500.

67. Ibid., pp. 497-500.

68. From Captain Andrew Geddes to General E.O.C. Ord, Commander of the Department of the Missouri, April 4, 1879. This letter is included in the report of Judge Advocate General Dunn.

69. Testimony of Captain Geddes, Geddes GCM (1879), RG 153, QQ 1387, Bx 1927, NA, pp. 481, 482.

70. Ibid., Information contained in request by the defense that Private G.W. Sweat be called as a defense witness, p. 631. This request was denied.

71. Testimony of Corporal George A. Hartford, Geddes GCM (1879), RG 153, QQ 1387, Bx 1927, NA, pp. 398, 406.

72. Report of Judge Advocate General Dunn to Secretary of War McCrory, Geddes GCM (1879), RG 153, QQ 1387, Bx 1927, NA.

73. Ibid., For full medical evidence, see the testimony of Dr. M.K. Taylor, pp. 245-247, 410; Testimony of Dr. John Moore, p. 260; and Testimony of Dr. George Cupples, pp. 411-415.

74. Ibid., Report of Judge Advocate General Dunn to Secretary of War McCrory.

75. Ibid.

76. Adjutant General's Office, General Court-Martial Orders, No. 66, (December 4, 1879), *Index of General Court-Martial Orders* (Washington: Adjutant General's Office, 1880), p. 2.

77. Heitman, *Historical Register and Dictionary*, Vol. 1, p. 760.

78. From Captain Andrew Geddes to General Absalom Baird, April 27, 1880, Geddes General Court-Martial (1880), Record Group 153, QQ 2020, Box 1970, National Archives.

79. Geddes GCM (1880), RG 153, QQ 2020, Box 1970, NA.

80. Merington, ed., *The Custer Story*, p. 194.

81. Thompson, "The Negro Soldier on the Frontier," *Journal of the West*, VII, 230.

82. Rudyard Kipling, "The Ladies," *Rudyard Kipling's Verse: Definitive Edition* (Garden City, New York: Doubleday and Company, 1946), p. 441.

Chapter 6
GLITTERING MISERY

1. Summerhayes, *Vanished Arizona*, p. 71.

BIBLIOGRAPHY

A. Primary Sources

1. Manuscripts and Unpublished Documents

Burt, Elizabeth J. "Forty Years in the Regular U.S. Army, 1862-1902." Manuscripts Division, Library of Congress, Washington, D.C.

Burt, Reynolds J. "Boyhood Data, 1874-1890." Don Rickey, Jr., Collection. Denver, Colorado.

Henry, Guy V., Jr. "A Brief Life of Guy V. Henry, Jr." U.S. Military History Research Collection. U.S. Army War College, Carlisle Barracks, Pennsylvania.

National Archives, Washington, D.C.

Records of the War Department

Office of the Adjutant General, Record Group 94.

Medical History of Camp Supply, September, 1868-February, 1893. Vol. 166 (September, 1868-February, 1877); Vol. 168 (February, 1877-February, 1882).

Medical History of Fort Stockton, Vol. 63 (May, 1869-October, 1872).

United States Army Continental Commands, 1821-1920, Record Group 393.

Letters Received, Fort Boise, 1864-1867.

United States Army Mobile Units, 1821-1942, Record Group 391.

Post and Regimental Order Book, Fort Totten, Headquarters of the 7th Cavalry, January, 1878-December, 1881.

Post Order Book, Fort Atkinson, Headquarters of the 6th Infantry, April 6, 1824.

Post Order Book, Fort Meade, January, 1887-November, 1887.

Sixth Infantry Orders, Fort Atkinson, October 8, 1823-October, 1824.

Office of the Judge Advocate General, General Court-Martial Records, Record Group 153.

149

Major Frederick Benteen (1887). RR 2327. Box 2271.
Private Andy Clayton (1874). PP 3995.
Colonel N.A.M. Dudley (1877). QQ 448. Drawer 61. Box 1866.
Lieutenant Henry O. Flipper (1882). QQ 2952. Boxes 2032, 2033.
Captain Thomas H. French (1879). QQ 994. Box 1902.
Captain Andrew Geddes (1879). QQ 1387. Box 1927.
——————— (1880). QQ 1554. Box 889.
Major Marcus A. Reno (1877). QQ 87. Drawer 60.
——————— (1880). QQ 1554. Box 889.
Captain George O. Sokalski (1866). MM 3975. Box 891.

Nickerson, Major A.H. "General Crook and the Indians: A Sketch." The Crook-Kennon Papers. U.S. Army Military History Institute. U.S. Army War College, Carlisle Barracks, Pennsylvania.

Paulding, Grace. "My Army Life." The William and Grace Paulding Papers. U.S. Military History Institute. U.S. Army War College, Carlisle Barracks, Pennsylvania.

Paulding, Colonel William. "A Few Words on My Army Life, From 1874-1913." The William and Grace Paulding Papers. U.S. Army Military History Institue. U.S. Army War College, Carlisle Barracks, Pennsylvania.

Sladen, Frederick W. "Childhood and Early Career Correspondences, 1874-1926." Sladen Family Papers. U.S. Army Military History Institute. U.S. Army War College, Carlisle Barracks, Pennsylvania. Pennsylvania.

Van Horn, James H. "The Frontier Army's Environment." Unpublished manuscript in the possession of Don Rickey, Jr., Denver, Colorado.

2. Diaries, Interviews, Letters

Mrs. Mary Julia Allen to Mrs. Carrie Riker, March 5, 1868. This is one of the "Letters of Lt. Colonel and Mrs. H.A. Allen." Compiled by Mrs. Victor R. Evans and on file at San Juan Island National Historic Site. Permission to use these letters granted by Ms. Patricia Milliren, Park Historian.

Sergeant Reginald Bradley, Grass Valley, California, January 10, 1968. Interview conducted by Don Rickey, Jr., for the National Park Service. Typescript available in the Don Rickey, Jr., Collection. Denver, Colorado.

Mrs. McCormack to Major L.H. Marshall, June 8, 1866. This letter is offered for sale by Don's Military Outpost, P.O. Box 63, Boston, Massachusetts.

Johnny O'Brien, Fort Laramie, Wyoming, April 4, 1961. Interview conducted by Jack McDermott, Rex Wilson, and Sally Johnson. Typescript available in the U.S. Army Military History Institute. U.S. Army War Colege, Carlisle Barracks, Pennsylvania.

Second Lieutenant Charles D. Rhodes. "Diary Notes of the Brulé-Sioux Indian Campaign, South Dakota, 1890-1891." Copy available in the U.S. Army Military History Institute. U.S. Army War College, Carlisle Barracks, Pennsylvania.

Captain Simon Snyder. "Diaries from 1866 through the 1880's." Loaned for copying by the Custer Battlefield National Monument, Crow Agency, Montana. Copied by Don Rickey, Jr. U.S. Army Military History Institute. U.S. Army War College, Carlisle Barracks, Pennsylvania.

Captain Simon Snyder to his mother, Mrs. M.C. Snyder, July 30, 1876, September 19, 1876. From the Snyder-Ronayne Collection. Custer Battlefield National Monument, Crow Agency, Montana. Copy available in the Don Rickey, Jr., Collection. Denver, Colorado.

Jake Tonamichel to Don Rickey, Jr., March 13, 17, 1957. Don Rickey, Jr., Collection. Denver, Colorado.

3. Government Publications

American State Papers, 1789-1838. 38 vols. Washington: Gales and Seaton, 1832-1861. *Military Affairs,* II, No. 199, 16 Cong., 2nd Sess. (1820), p. 211.

Heitman, Francis B. *Historical Register and Dictionary of the United States Army, 1789 to 1903.* 2 vols. Washington: Government Printing Office, 1903.

United States Congress. House of Representatives. *The Reorganization of the Army. House Report No. 354.* 44th Cong., 1st Sess. Washington: Government Printing Office, 1876.

――――――― *Reorganization of the Army: Report of a Sub-Committee on Military Affairs Relating to the Reorganization of the Army. House Miscellaneous Document No. 56.* 45th Cong., 2nd Sess. Washington: Government Printing Office, 1878.

War Department. *Annual Report of the Secretary of War, 1891.* 2 vols. Washington: Government Printing Office, 1891.

――――――― *Regulations for the Army of the United States and the General Orders in Force on the 17th of February, 1881.* Washington: Government Printing Office, 1881.

――――――― *Regulations for the Army of the United States, 1901.* Washington: Government Printing Office, 1902.

――――――― *Revised United States Regulations of 1861.* Washington: Government Printing Office, 1863.

――――――― Adjutant General's Office. *General Orders, Circulars and General Court-Martial Orders, 1883.* Washington: Government Printing Office, 1884.

――――――― *General Orders, Circulars and General Court-Martial Orders, 1887.* Washington: Government Printing Office, 1888.

――――――― *Index of General Court-Martial Orders, 1866.* Washington: Government Printing Office, 1867.

――――――― *Index of General Court-Martial Orders, 1877.* Washington: Government Printing Office, 1878.

――――――― *Index of General Court-Martial Orders, 1878.* Washington: Government Printing Office, 1879.

――――――― *Index of General Court-Martial Orders, 1879.* Washington: Government Printing Office, 1880.

――――――― *Index of General Court-Martial Orders, 1880.* Washington: Government Printing Office, 1881.

――――――― *Index of General Court-Martial Orders, 1882.* Washington: Government Printing Office, 1883.

_____ *Index of General Court-Martial Orders, 1887.* Washington: Government Printing Office, 1888.

_____ *Index of General Orders, 1861.* Washington: Government Printing Office, 1862.

_____ *Index of General Orders, 1870.* Washington: Government Printing Office, 1871.

_____ *Index of General Orders, 1878.* Washington: Government Printing Office, 1879.

_____ *Index of General Orders, 1881.* Washington: Government Printing Office, 1882.

_____ Surgeon General's Office. *Circular No. 4, A Report of Barracks and Hospitals with Descriptions of Military Posts, 1870.* Washington: Government Printing Office, 1870.

_____ *Circular No. 8, A Report of the Hygiene of the United States Army with Descriptions of the Military Posts.* Washington: Government Printing Office, 1875.

4. Newspapers

New York *World Telegram,* September 30, 1939.
Winners of the West, 1924.

5. Memoirs and Reminiscences

Anderson, Mrs. M.B. "A School Is Started in Old Fort Davis," *Women Tell the Story of the Southwest.* Compiled and edited by Mattie L. Wooten. San Antonio, Texas: The Naylor Company, 1940.

Biddle, Ellen McGowan. *Reminiscences of a Soldier's Wife.* Philadelphia: J.B. Lippincott Company, 1907.

Boyd, Mrs. Orsemus B. *Cavalry Life in Tent and Field.* New York: J. Selwin Tait and Sons, 1894.

Carrington, Frances C. *My Army Life and the Fort Phil. Kearney Massacre.* Philadelphia: J.B. Lippincott Company, 1910.

Carrington Margaret I. *Ab-Sa-Ra-Ka, Land of Massacre: Being the Experience of an Officer's Wife on the Plains.* Philadelphia: J.B. Lippincott and Company, 1879.

Custer, Elizabeth B. *Boots and Saddles or Life in Dakota with General Custer.* New York: Harper and Row, 1885.

_____ *Following the Guidon.* Norman: University of Oklahoma Press, 1966.

_____ *Tenting on the Plains or Gen'l Custer in Kansas and Texas.* New York: Charles L. Webster and Company, 1893.

De Trobriand, Philippe Régis Denis de Kerendern. *Vie Militaire dans le Dakota: Notes et Souvenirs, 1867-1869.* Paris: Librarie Ancienne, Honore Champion, 1924.

_____ Edited by Milo Quaife. Translated by George F. Will. Chicago: Lakeside Press, 1941.

FitzGerald, Emily McCorkle. *An Army Doctor's Wife on the Frontier: Letters from Alaska and the Far West, 1874-1878.* Edited by Abe Laufe. Pittsburgh: University of Pennsylvania Press, 1962.

Forsyth, Brigadier General George A. *The Story of a Soldier.* Vol. 1, *Builders of a Nation.* New York: D. Appleton and Company, 1900.

Fougera, Katherine G. *With Custer's Cavalry: From the Memoirs of the Late Katherine Gibson.* Caldwell, Idaho: The Caxton Printers, 1940.

Glisan, Rodney. *Journal of Army Life.* San Francisco: A.L. Bancroft and Company, 1874.

Hein, Lieutenant Colonel O.L. *Memoirs of Long Ago.* New York: G.P. Putnam's Sons, 1925.

La Guardia, Fiorello Henry. *The Making of an Insurgent, An Autobiography: 1882-1919.* Philadelphia: J.B. Lippincott Company, 1948.

Lane, Lydia Spenser. *I Married a Soldier or Old Days in the Old Army.* Philadelphia: J.B. Lippincott Company, 1893.

MacArthur, General Douglas. *Reminiscences.* New York: McGraw-Hill Book Company, 1964.

Mulford, Ami Frank. *Fighting Indians in the 7th United States Cavalry.* Corning, New York: Paul Lindsley Mulford, 1789.

Russell, Marian Sloan. *Land of Enchantment: Memoirs of Marian Russell Along the Santa Fé Trail.* Dictated to Mrs. Hal Russell. Edited by Garnet M. Bayer. Evanston, Illinois: The Branding Iron Press, 1954.

Roe, Frances M.A. *Army Letters from an Officer's Wife, 1871-1888.* New York: D. Appleton and Company, 1909.

Summerhayes, Martha. *Vanished Arizona: Recollections of the Army Life of a New England Woman.* Glorieta, New Mexico: The Rio Grande Press, 1970.

Ware, Captain Eugene F. *The Indian War of 1864.* Lincoln: University of Nebraska Press, 1965.

Zogbaum, Rufus F. *Horses, Foot, and Dragoon: Sketches of Army Life at Home and Abroad.* New York: Harper and Brothers, 1888.

6. Books

Glasson, William H. *Federal Military Pensions in the United States.* Edited by David Kinley. New York: Oxford University Press, 1918.

Moss, James A. *Officers' Manual (For use of subalterns).* Menosha, Wisconsin: Press of the George Banta Publishing Company, 1907.

7. Periodicals

Bourke, Captain John G. "Bourke on the Southwest." Edited by Lansing Bloom. *New Mexico Historical Review,* IX (April-July, 1934), 33-37, 159-183, 273-289.

——————. *New Mexico Historical Review,* X (January, 1935), 1-35.

Heistand, Mary Ripply. "Scraps from an Army Woman's Diary: An Old Army Christmas," *Army and Navy Life,* IX (December, 1907), 626-631.

Johnson, Roy P. "Jacob Horner of the 7th Cavalry," *North Dakota History,* XVI (April, 1949), 75-101.

Mattison, Ray H., ed. "An Army Wife on the Upper Missouri: The Diary of Sarah E. Canfield, 1866-1868," *North Dakota History,* XX (October, 1953), 191-220.

——————. "The Diary of Surgeon Washington Mathews," *North Dakota History,* XXI (January-April, 1934), 5-74.

Shields, Alice Mathews. "Army Life on the Wyoming Frontier," *Annals of Wyoming,* XIII (October, 1941), 331-343.

Walker, James F. "Old Fort Berthold as I Knew It," *North Dakota History*, XX (January, 1953), 25-45.

B. Secondary Sources

1. Books

Athearn, Robert G. *William Tecumseh Sherman and the Settlement of the West*. Norman: University of Oklahoma Press, 1956.

Brown, Dee. *The Gentle Tamers: Women of the Old Wild West*. G.P. Putnam's Sons, 1958.

Carriker, Robert C. *Fort Supply Indian Territory: Frontier Outpost on the Plains*. Norman: University of Oklahoma Press, 1970.

Compton, Piers. *Colonel's Lady and Camp-Follower: The Story of Women in the Crimean War*. New York: St. Martin's Press, 1970.

Dick, Everett. *Vanguards of the Frontier: A Social History of the Northern Plains and the Rocky Mountains*. New York: Tudor Publishing Company, 1941.

Dupuy, R. Ernest and Trevor N. Dupuy. *The Encyclopedia of Military History: From 3500 B.C. to the Present*. New York: Harper and Row, 1970.

Emmett, Chris. *Fort Union and the Winning of the Southwest*. Norman: University of Oklahoma Press, 1965.

Frink, Maurice and Casey Barthelmess. *Photographer on an Army Mule*. Norman: University of Oklahoma Press, 1965.

Graham, Colonel W.A. *The Custer Myth: A Source Book of Custeriana*. New York: Bonanza Books, 1953.

Griffin, Major Gerald E. *Ballads of the Regiment*. New York: George U. Harvey Publishing Company, 1918.

Leckie, William H. *The Buffalo Soldiers*. Norman: University of Oklahoma Press, 1967.

Mattes, Merrill J. *Indians, Infants and Infantry: Andrew and Elizabeth Burt on the Frontier*. Denver: The Old West Publishing Company, 1960.

Merington, Marguerite, ed. *The Custer Story: The Life and Intimate Letters of General George A. Custer and His Wife Elizabeth*. New York: The Devin-Adair Company, 1950.

Merrill, James M. *Spurs to Glory: The Story of the United States Cavalry*. New York: Rand McNally and Company, 1966.

Miles, Susan. *Fort Concho in 1877*. San Angelo, Texas: The Bradley Company, 1972.

Nye, Wilbur S. *Carbine and Lance: The Story of Old Fort Sill*. Norman: University of Oklahoma Press, 1937.

Rickey, Don, Jr. *Forty Miles a Day on Beans and Hay: The Enlisted Soldier Fighting the Indian Wars*. Norman: University of Oklahoma Press, 1963.

Rister, Carl Coke. *Fort Griffin on the Texas Frontier*. Norman: University of Oklahoma Press, 1956.

Terrell, John Upton and Colonel George Walton. *Faint the Trumpet Sounds: The Life and Trial of Major Reno*. New York: David McKay

Company, 1966.

Utley, Robert M. *Frontier Regulars: The United States Army and the Indian, 1866-1890.* New York: Macmillan Publishing Company, 1973.

Whitman, S.E. *The Troopers: An Informal History of the Plains Cavalry.* New York: Hastings House, 1962.

2. Periodicals

Dinges, Bruce J. "The Court-Martial of Lieutenant Henry O. Flipper: An Example of Black-White Relationships in the Army, 1881," *The American West,* IX (January, 1972), 12-16, 59-61.

McDermott, John Dishon. "Crime and Punishment in the United States Army: A Phase of Fort Laramie History," *Journal of the West,* VII (April, 1968), 246-255.

Mattison, Ray H. "The Army Posts on the Northern Plains, 1865-1885," *Nebraska History,* XXXV (March, 1954), 17-43.

Thompson, Edwin N. "The Negro Soldier on the Frontier: A Fort Davis Case Study," *Journal of the West,* VII (Arpil, 1968), 217-235.

3. Unpublished Dissertation and Theses

Burton, Wilfred C. "The Novels of Charles King, 1844-1933," Ph.D. dissertation, New York University, 1962.

Giese, Dale Frederick. "Social Life at Fort Union, New Mexico in the 1880's," Master's thesis, New Mexico Highlands University, 1964.

Welty, Raymond Leo. "The Western Army Frontier, 1860-1870," Ph.D. thesis, State University of Iowa, 1924.

INDEX

156

158